YUKON TERRITORY

ALASKA GEOGRAPHIC® / Volume 25, Number 2, 1998

To teach many more to better know and more wisely use our natural resources

About This Issue: Three writers living in the Yukon contributed to this issue on Alaska's northern neighbor. We thank Sarah Locke, Yvette Brend and John Steinbachs for their articles on various aspects of the Yukon's environment, people and lifestyle. To round out our coverage, we called on Dr. Donald W. Clark of Ontario for an account of the territory's prehistory, Dr. Norman E. Kagan of Minnesota for a review of early Westerners in Pelly River country and Dr. Frank Norris of Anchorage for a reminder that the movies' portrayal of the Yukon is often far from reality.

Several residents of the Yukon reviewed portions of the text and/or provided information, photos and maps for this issue. In particular, we thank John Ritter and the Yukon Native Language Center; Juri Peepre, president of the Canadian Parks and Wilderness Society; Ed Krahn of Tourism Yukon, who works with the Beringia Center in Whitehorse; Linda Bierlmeier and Jim Kemstead of Tourism Yukon; Dave Neufeld with Parks Canada and Craig Hart with the Yukon Geology Program; Jim McIntyre, director of Yukon Parks, and the staffs of the Dawson City Museum and Historical Society and of the Yukon Archives in Whitehorse. Candy Waugaman, a private historian and collector in Fairbanks, and Diane Brenner and Mina Jacobs of the Anchorage Museum provided important historical photos and documentation.

COVER: *Guide Joyce Majiski paddles one of the Yukon's many wilderness waterways.* (Cathie Archbould)

PREVIOUS PAGE: *Red fox kits play outside their den along the Dempster Highway.* (Don Cornelius)

FACING PAGE: *A storm clears from Mount Monolith in the Tombstone Mountains.* (Jon R. Nickles)

EDITOR
Penny Rennick

PRODUCTION DIRECTOR
Kathy Doogan

MARKETING DIRECTOR
Jill S. Brubaker

EDITORIAL ASSISTANT
Kerre Martineau

BOOKKEEPER
Claire Torgerson

POSTMASTER:
Send address changes to:

ALASKA GEOGRAPHIC®
P.O. Box 93370
Anchorage, Alaska 99509-3370

PRINTED IN U.S.A.

COLOR SEPARATIONS:
Graphic Chromatics

PRINTING:
Hart Press

ISBN: 1-56661-041-9

PRICE TO NON-MEMBERS THIS ISSUE: $21.95

BOARD OF DIRECTORS
Richard Carlson, Kathy Doogan, Penny Rennick

Robert A. Henning, **PRESIDENT EMERITUS**

ALASKA GEOGRAPHIC® (ISSN 0361-1353) is published quarterly by The Alaska Geographic Society, 639 West International Airport Rd., Unit 38, Anchorage, AK 99518. Periodicals postage paid at Anchorage, Alaska, and additional mailing offices. Copyright © 1998 by The Alaska Geographic Society. All rights reserved. Registered trademark: Alaska Geographic, ISSN 0361-1353; key title Alaska Geographic. This issue published March 1998.

THE ALASKA GEOGRAPHIC SOCIETY is a non-profit, educational organization dedicated to improving geographic understanding of Alaska and the North, putting geography back in the classroom and exploring new methods of teaching and learning.

MEMBERS RECEIVE *ALASKA GEOGRAPHIC®*, a high-quality, colorful quarterly that devotes each issue to monographic, in-depth coverage of a specific northern region or resource-oriented subject. Back issues are also available. Membership is $49 ($59 to non-U.S. addresses) per year. To order or request a free catalog of back issues, contact: Alaska Geographic Society, P.O. Box 93370, Anchorage, AK 99509-3370; phone (907) 562-0164, fax (907) 562-0479, e-mail: akgeo@aol.com.

SUBMITTING PHOTOGRAPHS: Those interested in submitting photos for possible publication should write for a list of upcoming topics or other photo needs and a copy of our editorial guidelines. We cannot be responsible for unsolicited submissions. Submissions not accompanied by sufficient postage for return by certified mail will be returned by regular mail.

CHANGE OF ADDRESS: The post office will not automatically forward *ALASKA GEOGRAPHIC®* when you move. To ensure continuous service, please notify us at least six weeks before moving. Send your new address and membership number or a mailing label from a recent issue of *ALASKA GEOGRAPHIC®* to: Alaska Geographic Society, Box 93370, Anchorage, AK 99509. If your book is returned to us by the post office because it is for some reason undeliverable, we will contact you to ask if you wish to receive a replacement for a small fee to cover additional postage.

The Library of Congress has cataloged this serial publication as follows:

Alaska Geographic. v.1-
   [Anchorage, Alaska Geographic Society] 1972-
   v. ill. (part col.). 23 x 31 cm.
   Quarterly
   Official publication of The Alaska Geographic Society.
   Key title: Alaska geographic, ISSN 0361-1353.

   1. Alaska–Description and travel–1959–
   –Periodicals. I. Alaska Geographic Society.

F901.A266 917.98'04'505 72-92087

Library of Congress 75[79112] MARC-S.

Contents

A Land of Dreams and Anguish 4

Lay of the Land 6

Kluane National Park 30

Other Parks and Protected Areas .. 40

Precontact History 50

Sara Abel of Old Crow 60

The Yukon's Mining Industry 68

Pelly Pioneers at Ross River 80

The Yukon in Celluloid 98

Today 104

Bibliography 125

Index 126

A Land of Dreams and Anguish

By Penny Rennick

In extreme northwestern North America sit a state and territory that could be sisters were it not for the vagaries of geography and an international boundary. Alaska and the Yukon Territory share this corner of the continent and often work in partnership to develop their economies.

But geography has always kept the two apart. Where Alaska sports an extensive coastline with major rivers providing arteries into its interior, the Yukon remains isolated behind an imposing mountain barrier. Little more than a century ago, Yukon-bound explorers had to travel cross-country from the heart of the continent or buck a current 1,400 miles (2,240 km.) from Alaska's Bering Sea coast up the Yukon River to circumvent the mountains. Only coastal Tlingit Indians routinely traversed the mountains to trade.

A wealth of furs and a veritable bonanza in gold shook the isolation of both Alaska and the Yukon. Beneath the gravels of the Yukon lay the lion's share of the gold, and the word "Klondike" sprang from the lips of fortune-seekers worldwide. To reach the gold, the prospectors needed access. This came with improved foot trails, expanded riverboat service and the White Pass & Yukon Route Railroad.

As the easy gold petered out, isolation again settled over the Yukon. It took a world war and another means of access, the Alcan Highway to stir the territory. The war gradually saw Whitehorse gain on Dawson City in prominence until it wrested the capital from the gold-rush boomtown.

For a time, riverboat traffic continued to provide passenger and freight service to the Yukon. But the boats could not compete with an improving highway route that spanned 1,500 miles (2,400 km.) from Dawson Creek, British Columbia, to Fairbanks, Alaska. The riverboats were dry-docked, highway traffic picked up as veterans sought a new life, and tiny communities blossomed around mining activity. But as the millennium approaches, urbanization remains mostly a dream, and perhaps not even that, for most Yukoners.

According to historian Dave Neufeld, the Yukon is one of the last places in the world where European culture came up against aboriginal cultures. The growing accommodation between those cultures has marked the Yukon ever since and from the earliest days, the lives of Westerners in the Yukon have revolved around those of the aboriginal groups, known in the 1990s as First Nations. Formal negotiations within this bicultural landscape have shaped government, mining, business and modern society. Biculturalism "has defined who we are here," says Neufeld.

Wilderness has also defined what Yukoners do there. And the territory wears its wildness well. It is a place of peace more than people, of wilderness more than Wall Street. But its ties with Alaska are strong and it is a worthy contributor to the mystique that resides in the northern frontier.

FACING PAGE: *The Yukon welcomes the McDougals (left) and Molly Chick of Alberta, Canada.* (Richard Montagna)

Lay of the Land

By Sarah Locke

Editor's note: *Sarah Locke is a freelance journalist living in Whitehorse.*

The distinctive outline of the Yukon Territory encloses 193,380 square miles (483,450 sq. km.) of wild scenic beauty. Walk the western border of the territory and you will traverse between the highest mountains in Canada and a sliver of beach on the Beaufort Sea. Wander the Yukon's interior and you'll find a land of rugged mountains, fast-flowing rivers and abundant wildlife.

The Yukon is named after the grandest of its many fast-flowing rivers, adopting the Gwitch'in name *Yu-kun-ah*, which means "great river." Originally the Yukon was part of the vast region called the Northwest Territories (NWT), which included all of the Canadian North as well as the prairie provinces of Alberta, Saskatchewan and Manitoba. The Klondike gold rush prompted the drawing of the Yukon's political boundaries in 1898.

Geographically, the Yukon has more in common with the interior forests and mountains of its western neighbor, Alaska, than with the barrenlands of the NWT to the east. All of the Yukon lies farther west than the coastal city of Vancouver, British Columbia. Beaver Creek on the Yukon/Alaska border is the westernmost community in Canada.

The famous stories of Yukon winters, immortalized by writers like Jack London and Robert Service, do not exaggerate the cold. The Yukon has a continental climate with long, cold winters. The lowest temperature recorded in North America, minus 81.4 degrees F (minus 63 C), was measured at Snag, Yukon, in February 1947. But it does warm up considerably in the summer. In fact, the Yukon has the greatest annual temperature range of any place on the continent. The difference between the average temperatures in the warmest and coldest months is around 104 degrees F (40 degrees C).

The massive coastal mountains block the regular passage of warmer Pacific air into the territory. They also trap precipitation, contributing to the Yukon's semiarid climate. Whitehorse, for example, receives about 10.6 inches (270 mm.) of precipitation per year. The Yukon's seven-month-long winters are generally dry as well as cold. Most of the precipitation falls in the summer as rain with July and August the wettest months.

The geographic diversity of the territory is striking. A subarctic plateau ranging in elevation from 300 to 4,500 feet (900 to 1,200 m.) makes up the bulk of the Yukon. This rough highland is punctuated by mountains, deep valleys and long, narrow lakes. In the north, the coastal plain slopes gently to the Beaufort Sea. Herschel, the

FACING PAGE: *Sheep Mountain overlooks Kluane Lake, largest in the territory, northwest of Haines Junction. (Don Cornelius)*

The Yukon's severe winters don't stop these Yukoners from creating an ice rink on the surface of Fox Lake north of Whitehorse. (Harry M. Walker)

Yukon's only island, lies just off this coast.

In the extreme southwest corner of the territory, Mount Logan dominates the Icefield Ranges of the St. Elias Mountains. At 19,550 feet (5,959 m.), Logan is the highest mountain in Canada and the second highest in North America. One of the earth's most massive mountains, Logan's summit plateau alone is 10 miles (16 km.) long.

The St. Elias Mountains form the highest coastal range in the world. Twenty peaks in this area tower more than 14,000 feet (5,000 m.) and from the summits of many, tidewater on the Pacific shore is visible. Storms from the Gulf of Alaska regularly envelop this area, feeding its mile-deep glaciers and forming the largest non-polar ice fields in the world.

The Yukon sports an abundance of mountains, in addition to the St. Elias giants. The Ogilvie, Wernecke and Selwyn mountains make up a broad band of sedimentary peaks running west to east across the middle northern Yukon. The Selwyn are the largest glaciated mountains in the Yukon outside of the St. Elias and parallel the dry Mackenzie Mountains, which form most of the territory's eastern border. The British and Richardson mountains in the extreme north represent the northernmost extension of the Rocky Mountain Cordillera in Canada. Near the territory's western border, granitic monoliths erupt into sharp, jagged peaks of the Tombstone Range. The profile of Tombstone Mountain is one of the Yukon's most recognizable landmarks.

Volcanism has also shaped the Yukon landscape. The most recent explosion occurred about 1,200 years ago, and the source of the ash has been traced to the Klutlan Glacier area just west of the Canadian border in the St. Elias Range. The white ash was dispersed widely over the southern Yukon, and can be clearly seen in soil profiles along many highway road cuts.

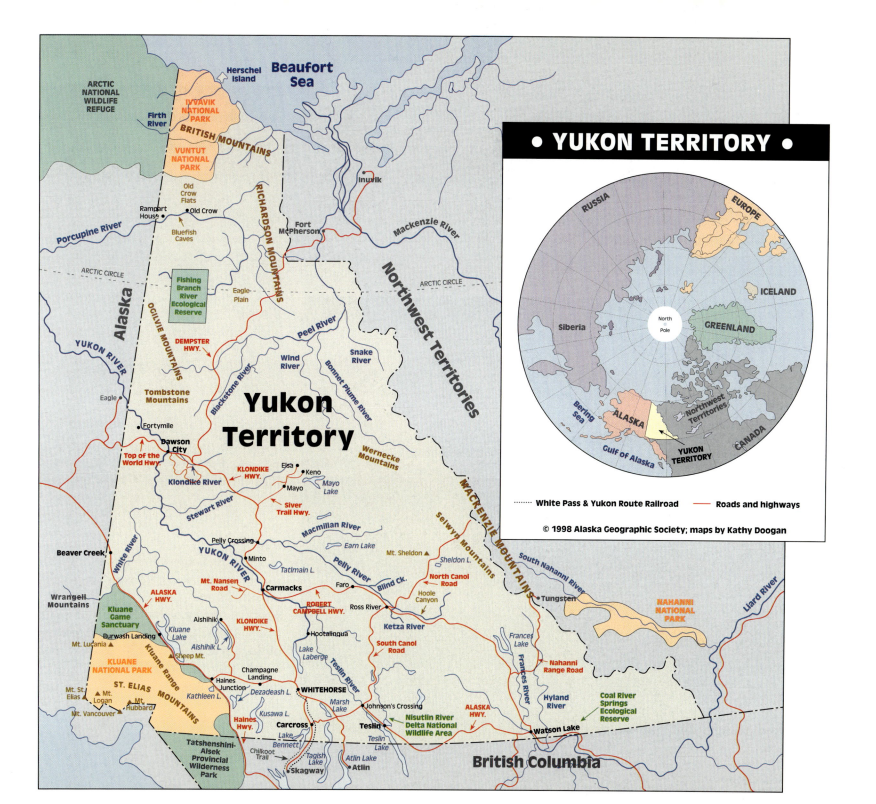

Two of the Western Cordillera's three major trenches are found in the Yukon. The Tintina Trench, longest of these wide, flat-bottomed valleys, starts in southcentral Yukon, and extends north and west for 450 miles (725 km.). In southwestern Yukon the smaller Shakwak Trench parallels the Tintina. Both of these rift valleys are important bird migration corridors.

The Yukon's complex geology has contributed to its heavy mineralization. But its most well-known mineral occurrence, the Klondike gold fields, owes its existence as much to an ice-age anomaly as to geologic forces. Glaciers never scoured the Klondike, so its incredibly rich deposits of placer gold were left concentrated in a relatively small area.

A myriad of fast, free-flowing rivers have carved their way through the Yukon's mountains and plateaus. The Yukon River, which starts on a high plateau in the southern part of the Yukon and drains three-quarters of the territory, is the fifth longest river in North America. It arcs westward for 1,980 miles (3,185 km.), crossing Alaska before emptying into the Bering Sea. Major Yukon tributaries include the Teslin, 245 miles

The North Fork of the Klondike River flows through the Tintina Trench, a rift valley arcing across portions of the Yukon and Alaska. (George Wuerthner)

• Yukon Relativity •

Yukoners enjoy comparing the territory's small number of people with its abundant numbers of wildlife. Using this Yukon Relativity Scale, there are two moose for every Yukoner and one grizzly for every five Yukoners.

The comparison also extends to the amount of wilderness Yukoners have to enjoy. The territory's land mass accounts for 4.9 percent of Canada. The territory's population, at about 33,000, accounts for less than 1 percent of Canada's 30 million citizens. If Yukoners evenly dispersed themselves throughout the territory, each man, woman and child could surround themselves with about 6 square miles (15 sq. km.) of land. ●

Five Finger Rapids, an infamous marker to early gold-seekers, awaits travelers on the Yukon downriver from Whitehorse. (George Matz)

(393 km.); Pelly, 378 miles (608 km.); White, 199 miles (320 km.); Stewart, 305 miles (488 km.) and the Porcupine, about 555 miles (888 km.), most of which flows through Alaska.

The Yukon River has been an important travel route for thousands of years and during the Klondike gold rush, more than 30,000 sourdoughs raced down the waterway to reach Dawson City. Once the rush ended, sternwheelers continued a busy trade along the river, serving many Yukon communities, until the road system replaced the river as the primary transportation route.

Now more people float the Yukon than any other waterway in the North. The river is easily navigable between Whitehorse and its mouth for those few months of the year that it is not frozen over. The Miles Canyon rapids that capsized many a Klondike sourdough were drowned by a reservoir when the Whitehorse dam was built in 1957.

• MAMMALS OF THE YUKON •

ABOVE: *Southern Yukon provides suitable habitat for elk. (Larry Anderson)*

ABOVE RIGHT: *A longer, more slender face distinguishes mountain goat from Dall sheep. (George Wuerthner)*

RIGHT: *Black bears inhabit forested areas of the Yukon. (Alissa Crandall)*

FACING PAGE: *Symbol of the wild, the wolf still finds a home in many areas of the Yukon. (Larry Anderson)*

BELOW: *This grizzly forages among lowland slopes of Kluane National Park.* (Richard Montagna)

RIGHT: *Pikas, members of the rabbit family, scamper among rocky slopes of central and southern Yukon.* (Robert Hahn)

BELOW RIGHT: *Powered by a ferocious appetite, this short-tailed weasel attacks a caribou tenderloin.* (Robert Hahn)

FACING PAGE: *Dall sheep enjoy the sunny slopes of Sheep Mountain.* (Cathie Archbould)

ABOVE: *In central Yukon Territory, the Yukon River flows through a broad valley, with parts of its channel flanked by steep bluffs where peregrine falcons nest. (Craig Flatten)*

LEFT: *Whitehorse is nestled in a curve of the Yukon River. The Robert Campbell Bridge spans the river, passing by the hospital at lower right. (Cathie Archbould)*

In Yukon Territory, the river runs through a wide, forested valley, coursing through several major lakes and winding between extensive river terraces. One stretch of the river, the 30-Mile section downriver from Whitehorse, is identified as a Canadian Heritage River.

The Peel River in northeastern Yukon, named for a former British prime minister, served as one of the first gateways to the region for European explorers. The wild waters of Aberdeen Canyon along its upper section are unrunnable, but farther downstream the Peel turns slow and muddy as it flows between high-graveled cliffs and lowlands of stunted spruce. The Peel flows east and north before joining the Mackenzie, Canada's largest river.

At least twice during the Pleistocene Epoch, which ended about 10,000 years ago, glaciers blocked the eastward flow of the Peel and diverted the river west into the Yukon River. It appears that some species of fish indigenous to the Yukon River were trapped in the Peel at this time. At least six species of fish now found in the Peel are considered to be relict populations from the Yukon River or ones that developed in unglaciated portions of the Peel. These fish, which differ genetically from species in the Mackenzie River system, include northern pike, arctic grayling and lake trout.

Six major tributaries join the Peel in Yukon Territory, one of which, the Bonnet Plume, is the newest of the Yukon's heritage rivers. The Wind, Snake and Bonnet Plume, among the most well-known of these tributaries, start high in the Wernecke Mountains and descend swiftly to the Peel River Basin. They range between 124

• FAST FACTS •

Territorial size:
  193,380 sq. mi. (483,450 sq. km.)
Inland waters:
  1,792 sq. mi. (4,481 sq. km.)
Population:
  33,586 (Source: Yukon Government)
  (1996 census recorded 30,766)
Capital:
  Whitehorse, population 24,031
  (Source: Yukon Government)
Flower: Fireweed
Bird: Raven
Gemstone: Lazulite
Longest river:
  Yukon River, 1,980 mi. (3,185 km.)
Highest mountain:
  Mount Logan, 19,550 ft. (5,959 m.)
Largest lake:
  Kluane Lake, 154 sq. mi. (400 sq. km.)

creating a fantastic series of fragile tufa formations. A territorial park now protects the area, but getting there is not easy. There is no road access.

Another distinctive water feature is the series of long, linear lakes that fringe part of southern Yukon. All oriented north to south, the basins holding these lakes were caused by glaciation. The lakes are as much as 60 miles (100 km.) long and several extend south into British Columbia. These lakes, such as Teslin, Atlin, Tagish, Bennett, Marsh, Kusawa and Laberge, are important staging areas for waterfowl. One of the first signs of spring in the Yukon is the arrival of thousands of swans that congregate on ice-free sections of the lakes before migrating farther north to nesting grounds.

About 3 percent of the Yukon is covered by wetlands, a lower percentage than in most parts of Canada. Forty-eight wetlands have been identified as significant for migratory

and 186 miles (200-300 km.) in length.

The Liard, the territory's other major river, drains the Yukon's entire southeast corner and continues flowing southeast before emptying into the Mackenzie, which then flows north to the Beaufort Sea. The Liard Plain forms a break in the mountains more than 124 miles (200 km.) wide. Major tributaries of the Liard include the Hyland, Frances and Coal rivers. One of Canada's most unusual thermal springs is perched on a terrace above the Coal where cool spring water seeps over the edge of a limestone cliff,

The Yukon's clear waters attract fishermen and outdoor enthusiasts. This pair of kayakers patrol Lake Laberge. (Harry M. Walker)

FACING PAGE: *Among the most famous images of the Yukon, the granite spires of the Tombstone Mountains, shown here reflecting in Grizzly Lake, arrest travelers along the Dempster Highway. Igneous rocks intruded the sedimentary layers of the Ogilvie Mountains to produce these dramatic peaks. The Yukon government is studying the core area of the Tombstones to determine if they will establish a park to protect the area.* (Laurent Dick)

RIGHT: *The 144-mile (230 km.) North Canol Road passes through this valley in eastern Yukon Territory. The road runs from the territory's border with the Northwest Territories to the community of Ross River where the road joins the South Canol Road and continues to the Alaska Highway at Johnson's Crossing.* (Laurent Dick)

bird habitat, and some are internationally significant. The most extensive wetlands are north of the Arctic Circle on flat, poorly drained land.

Old Crow Basin in northwest Yukon contains some of the most important wildlife habitat in the territory. The hills and pediment slopes of this huge, bowl-shaped area once enclosed an ancient glacial lake. When the lake drained, it created a vast lacustrine plain now known as Old Crow Flats. The flats are dotted with more than 2,000 shallow lakes and ponds and in the summer, as many as half a million birds use this wetland for breeding and molting. This nesting habitat is particularly important when drought dries up alternate nesting sites on the Canadian prairies.

Old Crow Flats serves all four of the major flyways in North America. Ducks such as greater and lesser scaup, white-winged scoter, green-winged teal, northern pintail and American wigeon are the most abundant waterfowl. Common, Pacific and red-throated loons, horned grebes, greater white-fronted geese and tundra swans also use the flats. Tundra swans cross all the way from the Atlantic Flyway to breed here.

The Old Crow Basin is part of a vast, unglaciated region called Beringia. When glaciers covered most of the continent during the last major ice age, this dry land served as a refuge for many plants and animals. Beringia included much of central and northern Yukon, and stretched west across Alaska to eastern Siberia via a land bridge. This land link across Bering Strait was formed when sea levels dropped because huge quantities of seawater were frozen into massive glaciers. Pleistocene animals, birds and insects crossed this land bridge to North America, as did nomadic hunters.

• BIRDS OF THE YUKON •

ABOVE: *White-tailed ptarmigan inhabit the Tombstone Mountains.* (Jon R. Nickles)

ABOVE RIGHT: *Black guillemot perch among the weathered buildings of Herschel Island.* (Laurent Dick)

RIGHT: *A young gyrfalcon announces its first kill.* (Robert Hahn)

LEFT: *These rufous hummingbird fledglings are about to leave their crowded nest.* (Robert Hahn)

BELOW: *A mountain bluebird brightens a summer day at Whitehorse.* (Tom Soucek)

BELOW: *This view from Sapper Hill overlooks the Yukon wilderness crossed by the Dempster Highway. The hill's name is a nickname for an army engineer and honors the 3rd Royal Canadian Engineers, who built the bridge spanning the Ogilvie River.* (Edward Steele)

RIGHT: *The Blackstone Uplands offer some of the best opportunities to see wildlife in northcentral Yukon.* (Karen Cornelius)

Cold and arid, Beringia was clothed in hardy grasses, herbs, dwarf birch and willows. This rich plant life supported woolly mammoth, mastodon, steppe bison, giant ground sloths, giant beavers, and North American horses and camels. At the top of the food chain were predators such as giant short-faced bears, lions and scimitar cats.

Today Old Crow Flats is a treasure house for the remains of these extinct mammals. Known as the richest paleontological area in Canada for ice-age mammals, more than 20,000 fossils have been collected here. Most have been patiently dug from the permafrost banks of the Old Crow River.

Just 40 miles (65 km.) southwest of Old Crow Basin lies one of the most famous archaeological sites in the Americas. Archaeologists working at Bluefish Caves think that they have found bone tools used by humans as much as 24,000 years ago. If these dates can be confirmed, Bluefish Caves would hold some of the earliest evidence of humans in the New World.

North of Old Crow Basin, beyond the British Mountains, is the gently sloping plain of the Yukon's northern coast. This is the territory's only "low arctic" habitat. Permafrost lies close beneath the surface, limiting plant growth. Tussock fields of sedge and cottongrass, mixed with forbs, lichens and mosses, cover most of the land.

About 15 percent of the Yukon lies above the Arctic Circle, the imaginary line that rings the earth at approximately 66 degrees 33 minutes N. This is the latitude at which the sun never sets on June 21, the longest day of the year. The Yukon's Dempster Highway is one of only two public roads in North America that cross the Arctic Circle.

Permafrost, permanently frozen ground, becomes continuous about 75 miles (120 km.) north of the Arctic Circle, above the Porcupine River. This frozen ground is discontinuous but widespread throughout the rest of the territory and its thickness varies with latitude. Along the northern coast, permafrost has been measured at 785 feet (238 m.) deep; in the southern Yukon, discontinuous patches of permafrost might be only 6.6 feet (2 m.) deep.

The Yukon's forests are well-adapted to this cold soil. About 60 percent of the Yukon is forested, and most of these trees are part of the boreal forest, that vast belt of conifers that encircles the Northern Hemisphere. Subarctic forest or taiga gives way to tundra farther north. The most productive forests are found in the south, where industrial logging has spawned a new industry.

LEFT: *Because of its location in northwestern North America, portions of Yukon Territory were incorporated within a prehistoric area known as Beringia, a wide land bridge linking Asia and North America. Much of Beringia was unglaciated during the ice ages of the Pleistocene Epoch, which allowed prehistoric mammals to migrate and flourish throughout the region. To celebrate this rich fauna, Yukoners built Beringia Centre near Whitehorse, where this skeleton of a woolly mammoth is exhibited. (Yukon Government)*

ABOVE: *These show gardens near Whitehorse display arrangements of many northern flower species. (Harry M. Walker)*

ABOVE: *Wind and weathering have created this small dune field of glacial silt near Carcross. (Chlaus Lotscher)*

RIGHT: *Although limited by their homeland's climate, some Yukoners have managed to raise feed crops. This ranch near Dezadeash Lake provides hay for horses in the Kluane area. (Richard Montagna)*

The Yukon's trees make up about 5 percent of Canada's forests. Common tree species are white and black spruce, lodgepole pine, aspen and balsam poplar. At higher elevations the main species are alpine fir in southcentral and eastern Yukon and white spruce in western and northern areas. Along the Firth River, white spruce grow farther north than anywhere else in Canada, reaching within 19 miles (30 km.) of the Beaufort Sea.

Fire is a regular part of this forest ecosystem. On average Yukon forests burn every 80 to 200 years. Prized morel mushrooms are one of the first species to poke through the ash after a forest fire.

Another species that thrives in disturbed areas is the vibrant fireweed, the Yukon's territorial flower, which lines roadsides throughout the North. The territory also has rarer plants, survivors of the Ice Age in Beringia, about 30 species of which occur only in the Yukon or here and in neighboring parts of Alaska.

Agriculture in the Yukon is a challenge, and climate is the major constraint. The number of frost-free days ranges from about 21 in Haines Junction near Kluane National Park to 75 around Dawson City. Killing frosts can occur any month of the year, but Yukon farmers and gardeners have always taken pride in beating the elements. During the gold rush, local market gardens produced most of the vegetables and forage crops needed to feed the 30,000 residents then living in Dawson City. Today the amount of land under production continues to increase.

About 40 square miles (100 sq. km.) of land have been developed for farming. In the most productive areas, barley, oats, hay and a range of vegetables can be grown, but most of the lands being farmed are suitable only for forage crops and cool climate vegetables.

With little farming, few roads and a forest industry still in its infancy, the Yukon remains a wild land. Three-quarters of the territory is considered wilderness, and wildlife populations are generally in good shape. The large predators exterminated in most of North America still have a home here. About 6,000 to 7,000 grizzly bears roam the territory. Black bears, which number around 10,000, are found in forested areas. More than 4,500 wolves are spread throughout the Yukon and wolverine populations are healthy.

The 60,000 moose in the territory outnumber Yukoners almost two to one. They are part of what biologists sometimes call the "spruce-moose" biome. Small numbers of mule deer and elk are found in the southern Yukon. About 150 muskoxen live on the North Slope. Caribou, that most northern of ungulates, are found in scattered herds across the territory. The Yukon has about 30,000 woodland caribou and one great migratory herd of barrenground caribou. The 170,000 animals in the Porcupine caribou herd range across northern Yukon and into northeast Alaska. They calve along the coastal plain of the Yukon/Alaska border.

The Yukon's roster of endangered species includes the bowhead whale and the peregrine falcon, whose numbers have rebounded dramatically in the territory during

As the largest population center in the Yukon, bustling Whitehorse offers amenities found in many urban areas. (Harry M. Walker)

Watson's General Store at Carcross carries on the tradition of one-stop-shopping pioneered by general stores of an earlier time. This outlet focuses on tourism and stocks just about any item related to the Yukon designed to catch the visitor's eye. (Harry M. Walker)

LEFT: *This view from the Weisshorn in the St. Elias Mountains shows mounts Vancouver, Hubbard and Alverstone, all topping 14,000 feet (4,246 m.), at center and right, fronting a vista of giants St. Elias (18,008 feet; 5462 m.) and Logan (19,550 feet; 5959 m.) to the left. (Chlaus Lotscher)*

BELOW LEFT: *East of Kluane National Park, the immense peaks of the Icefield Ranges give way to a gentler terrain, depicted by these hills north of Dezadeash Lake. (Craig Flatten)*

FACING PAGE: *Fall colors brighten a southwestern Yukon landscape. (Edward Steele)*

the last decade. Wood bison, a threatened species, were reintroduced to the Yukon in 1986.

There are about 22,000 thinhorn sheep in the Yukon, more than anywhere else in Canada. Thinhorn sheep include both Dall and stone sheep. About 1,700 mountain goats are concentrated in the southern third of the territory.

Four species of Pacific salmon are found here. The chinook salmon that swim nearly 2,000 miles (3,200 km.) up the Yukon River from the Bering Sea make the longest migration of this species in the world. Dolly Varden charr are found in rivers on the North Slope, and fresh water supports populations of lake trout, whitefish, northern pike and burbot.

Thirteen raptor and six owl species

make the Yukon their home. These include peregrine and gyrfalcons, great gray and short-eared owls and bald eagles. Thirty-four species of swans, geese and ducks spend at least part of their year in the Yukon. Dozens of migratory bird species are seasonal visitors.

Off the northern coast, the marine mammal inventory includes ringed and bearded seals and the endangered bowhead whale. Polar bears sometimes den on Herschel Island.

The mammals and birds of the Yukon inhabit one of North America's most beautiful and pristine landscapes. It is a powerful land, where long, dark winters and brilliant summers give a strong pulse to the yearly cycle of life. From its mountains and rivers, to its herds of caribou and packs of wolves, the Yukon remains a wild land where nature takes center stage. ●

• PLANTS OF THE YUKON •

ABOVE: *Fireweed lives up to its name as the colors of autumn tinge its leaves.* (Laurent Dick)

ABOVE RIGHT: *Golden rays of sun illuminate this field of foxtail.* (Laurent Dick)

RIGHT: *Poplar leaves contrast with this patch of highbush cranberry leaves in southern Yukon.* (George Wuerthner)

ABOVE: *Barring disaster, this lodgepole pine seedling can look forward to a long life in the southern Yukon.* (Laurent Dick)

RIGHT: *Spores of the bird's nest fungi explode from the "eggs" when raindrops fall on this unique species.* (Robert Hahn)

Kluane National Park

By Sarah Locke

In the southwest corner of the Yukon, the massive peaks of Kluane National Park dominate a world of ice and snow. The Icefield Ranges of the St. Elias Mountains have the largest concentration of high peaks in North America. Immense rivers of ice, streaked with glacial moraines, flow in every direction, forming one of the largest non-polar ice fields in the world.

Ice-capped mountains and glaciers cover more than 80 percent of Kluane, but the park also has a less frigid side. As the massive glaciers emerge from the mountains and reach the lowlands, they melt and feed the lakes and rivers in Kluane's lowlands. This ribbon of life along the eastern edge of the park protects the most unusual and varied mix of plants and wildlife found anywhere in northern Canada.

The park's life-giving buffer would not exist without the extreme land beyond it; the high mountains and massive ice fields that create their own violent storms; the surging glaciers that still carve the landscape. Kluane, a land of extremes and superlatives, stands out as one of Canada's most prized national parks.

The most prominent feature of Kluane lies well hidden in the heart of the park. At 19,550 feet (5,959 m.), Logan is the highest mountain in Canada and the second highest peak on the continent. Some of the world's biggest valley glaciers descend from its flanks, huge rivers of ice that flow for 62 miles (99 km.) to tidewater on the Pacific.

Anchored alone in the middle of its ice fields, Mount Logan is among the most massive mountains in the world when measured around its base. Its 10-mile-long plateau preceding the summit has discouraged many a climber. Lower down, the mountain stretches for 24 miles from east to west. Expeditions have spent many weeks just skiing around the mountain.

Mount Logan crowns one of the most dynamic landscapes to be found anywhere in North America. The St. Elias Mountains are the youngest major range in Canada, and the earth's crust is still active here. The Pacific and North American plates, two of the earth's 20-odd tectonic plates, collide beneath the ice fields, grinding against one another and forcing these mountains skyward by a few inches every year.

More than 2,000 glaciers hang off the mountains. They're fed by violent storms that blow in from the Pacific and drop as much as 28 inches (700 mm.) of precipitation per year on the ice fields. As the snow compacts into ice, its weight forces the glaciers to creep downhill. Occasionally they surge wildly, galloping forward at a rate that's visible to the naked eye. In the 1960s, Steele Glacier traveled more than five miles (eight km.) in two years, advancing at a rate of about 1 yard (.91 m.) per hour.

FACING PAGE: *A three-dimensional map provides a bird's-eye view of Kluane National Park at the visitor center at Haines Junction. (Chlaus Lotscher)*

Rafters confront one of several glaciers that drain into the Alsek River as the waterway breaches the coastal mountains, joins with the Tatshenshini River and empties into the Gulf of Alaska at Dry Bay. (Joyce Majiski)

These massive glaciers feed the only river powerful enough to breach the ramparts of the coastal mountains. The Alsek River was already threading its way to the Pacific before the major periods of uplift began. As the mountains continued their rise skyward, the river kept pace by cutting deep gorges. Within the depths of Turnback Canyon, along the British Columbia portion of the river, some of the wildest whitewater on the continent unleashes its fury.

Upstream of Turnback, Lowell Glacier calves giant icebergs directly into the river. At least five times in the last thousand years, Lowell Glacier has surged across the Alsek, blocking it and creating a massive glacial lake.

About 150 years ago, the most recent ice dam broke in one cataclysmic event, releasing a towering wall of water that swept the river valley below, scouring the hillsides. Native stories tell of a group of Tlingits, camped at the junction of the Alsek and Tatshenshini rivers, who were drowned in the flood. Today the Alsek Valley still bears the marks of these glacial lakes. Long hillside benches high up the mountainsides show where waves once lapped the shore, and driftwood marks the site of former beaches.

The Alsek rises beneath the Kluane Range in the eastern part of the park. Rising abruptly to heights of 8,000 feet (2,426 m.), these mountains are influenced by both Pacific and Arctic air masses. Their alpine meadows and forested valleys support a wide range of plants, with species characteristic of the coast, the Arctic, the western mountains, the northern prairies and the steppes of Asia.

Extensive forests of white spruce, trembling aspen and balsam poplar cover the lower slopes and valleys. Higher up willow, dwarf birch and alder form the transition to the tundra. In summer the land above the trees explodes with color with arctic poppies, purple saxifrage, mountain heather and moss campion all contributing to the intense, but short-lived display.

Kluane supports an unusually high diversity of large mammals for such a northern latitude. Many species are either at or near the northern or southern limit of their range in North America. Dall sheep, the most abundant large mammal in the park, feed on alpine grasses high on the mountain slopes. Most of the Yukon's mountain goats live among the rocky ridges in the southern part of the park. Moose browse in the willow thickets.

Between 150 and 400 grizzlies range through the park, denning in alpine and subalpine areas and moving lower in the summer to feed on soapberries (buffaloberries) and bear root. Black bears live in the forests and wolves hunt in the lowlands.

Other wildlife found in Kluane include wolverine, muskrat, mink, marmot, red fox, lynx, otter, coyote, beaver, snowshoe hare and arctic ground squirrel. Kokanee salmon, a land-locked form of sockeye salmon, swim the waters of Kathleen Lake.

Surprisingly enough, the legendary ice worm is not the only animal that lives in the heart of the ice fields. Pikas live in tiny meadows on isolated nunataks, islands of rock that stick up out of the ice cap. Young pikas travel as much as 6 miles (9.6 km.) over the ice to find unoccupied meadows on other nunataks.

These small herbivores normally live among rocky talus slopes, dashing out to nearby meadows to harvest grasses. In the ice fields there is never enough grass to go around, so the pikas have found another food source. Violent storms often blow birds onto the ice fields. The pikas scurry onto the ice to collect the dead birds, and then eat their brains, a welcome source of fat for animals that do not hibernate.

Kluane's greenbelt provides a more welcoming habitat for birds. About 118 species nest in the park alone. In a single day sightings could include rock ptarmigan and wandering tattlers, mountain bluebirds, hawk owls, golden eagles and yellow-rumped warblers.

At 8,500 square miles (22,100 sq. km.), Kluane is Canada's largest mountain park, but it is just one part of a much larger wilderness. Wrangell-St. Elias National Park, the largest national park in the United States, wraps around Kluane to the west and the southwest. Southeast of Kluane on the Alaska coast is Glacier Bay National Park and Preserve.

In 1993 British Columbia inserted the missing piece into this wilderness puzzle by establishing Tatshenshini-Alsek Wilderness

Highest point in Canada, Mount Logan (19,550 feet, 5,959 m.) towers over Mount Hubbard and neighboring peaks in the St. Elias Mountains. (Chlaus Lotscher)

Provincial Park. This key area protects the lands and the rivers between Kluane and Glacier Bay. The four parks protect 25 million acres or 39,000 square miles (101,400 sq. km.), a region the size of the state of Kentucky. These parklands form the largest international protected area in the world and are recognized jointly as a UNESCO World Heritage Site.

Kluane, a Southern Tutchone word meaning "place of many fish," refers to the waters of the Yukon's largest lake. The Southern Tutchone traditionally lived along the lakes and rivers of the Kluane region, building their culture on the rich wildlife resources of this land. They traded with the Tlingits on the coast, but had little contact with non-Natives until the late 1800s.

FACING PAGE: *Kluane National Park joins with British Columbia's Tatshenshini-Alsek Wilderness Provincial Park and Alaska's Glacier Bay and Wrangell-St. Elias national parks to form the largest international protected area in the world. As early as 1979 UNESCO had designated lands within Kluane and Wrangell-St. Elias a world heritage area. Subsequently, the entire protected region has been classified as a world heritage site.* (Richard Montagna)

BELOW: *Rock Glacier Trail climbs the benchlands west of the Haines Highway to provide this overview of Dezadeash Lake.* (George Wuerthner)

FAR RIGHT: *A beaver pond along the Dezadeash River frames the Auriol Range in Kluane National Park.* (George Wuerthner)

In 1896, Jack Dalton, an Oklahoma cowboy and logger, improved a Native trading route that ran south of the park. This colorful character declared the Dalton Trail a toll road, and supplied the Klondikers who followed this route to the Dawson goldfields. A minor gold rush drew more people to the Kluane area in 1903.

World War II brought major changes to the Kluane area and to all of the Yukon. In 1942, fearing a Japanese invasion, the U.S. and Canadian governments decided to ram a road through the northern wilderness to serve as a military supply line to Alaska. Soon American soldiers were bulldozing a route through the valleys beneath the Kluane Range.

The soldiers were allowed to hunt in the Yukon, leading to concerns about protection of the territory's wildlife. Just weeks after the Alaska Highway was officially opened, the Canadian government set aside land for the Kluane Game Sanctuary. Kluane was established as a national park reserve in 1972, pending settlement of land claims in the Yukon.

The Alaska and Haines highways parallel the park's eastern border, and present

dramatic views of the rugged Kluane Range. In a few places along the road one can catch glimpses of the peaks in the interior of the park, but the Kluane Range is substantial enough that it blocks most views of the icefield giants to the west.

The St. Elias Mountains attract climbers and ski mountaineers from around the world, drawn by the concentration of high peaks there. Now most adventurers fly into the ice fields, but the first climbers to explore these mountains walked in from the coast. Mount St. Elias (18,005 feet; 5,461 m.), the huge peak that can be seen from the Gulf of Alaska, lured them into the ice fields.

St. Elias, the third highest peak on the

ABOVE LEFT: *A climber studies the Weisshorn from Mount Poland in the Cathedral Glacier area of the park. (Chlaus Lotscher)*

FAR LEFT: *Spring buds look to a new year at Kathleen Lake, about 30 miles (48 km.) south of Haines Junction. (Matt McGovern-Rowen)*

NEAR LEFT: *Louie Janssen gets up close and personal with this iceberg in Lowell Lake in the Alsek drainage. Icebergs can shift and approaching them requires caution. (Joyce Majiski)*

FACING PAGE: *Climbers set up base camp on Hubbard Glacier during an ascent of Mount Logan, partially wrapped in clouds. (Laurent Dick)*

continent, was first climbed in 1897 by an Italian team led by the Duke of Abruzzi. The wealthy aristocrat, not one to forego his luxuries, had porters drag his brass bed into the base camp on the ice fields. When Mount Logan was first climbed in 1925, it took the climbers six weeks just to ferry their supplies to the base of the remote mountain.

There are many opportunities for exploring Kluane's less forbidding greenbelt area. Birders often choose the Dezadeash River Wetlands Trail, one of three self-guiding

interpretive trails in the park. The Auriol Trail, one of the longer established trails, ascends to alpine meadows in a 12-mile (19.2-km.) loop. The steep hike up Sheep Mountain offers a good chance of seeing the Dall sheep that feed on its south-facing slopes.

Some routes, such as the Slims River hike and the Cottonwood Trail, follow abandoned mining roads. Mountain biking is allowed on the old road to Alsek Pass, which is also passable with four-wheel drive vehicles. From the rocky knoll at the pass there are sweeping views of the Alsek Valley and the Kluane Range. Nearby is Thunder Egg Creek, which is named after unique spherical concretions, formed by glacial processes, which wash out of the cliffs upstream.

Many of the longer hikes are wilderness routes involving stream crossings and route finding, and are recommended for experienced backpackers only. All hikers in Kluane are asked to remember that bears make their homes in the park, and people are the transient visitors.

Rafting the Alsek River, a Canadian Heritage River, offers another superb way to experience the park. Grizzly bears are often seen during the three-to-four-day trip as the Alsek Valley is prime grizzly habitat. Most groups end their adventure with a hike up Goatherd Mountain, and then fly out from Lowell Lake, a widening of the river below the terminus of Lowell Glacier. Traveling the full length of the river to the Pacific Ocean requires an expensive helicopter portage around Turnback Canyon.

There are many different ways to experience Kluane, from climbing its highest peaks to investigating a meadow of wildflowers. But every Kluane encounter has one common denominator: Any trip here guarantees visitors a chance to see wilderness at its very best. ●

FACING PAGE: *White sediment on the lake bottom combines with low oxygen levels to create this milky effect in Emerald Lake along the Klondike Highway. (Chlaus Lotscher)*

RIGHT: *Waves lap the shore of Kluane Lake. The Alaska Highway follows the west shore of the lake for about 40 miles (64 km.). (Laurent Dick)*

Other Parks and Protected Areas

By Sarah Locke

The Yukon is still a wild place. In this northern land you can travel for weeks without seeing another soul or crossing a road. Only 33,000 people live in a territory larger than the state of California. Even in Whitehorse, where most Yukoners live, wild country can be found not far from most people's doorsteps.

About 8 percent of Yukon lands are protected, and these areas represent an array of ecosystems. They range from the fragile tufa formations of Coal River Springs to the wetlands of Old Crow Flats, the coastal plain of Ivvavik National Park and the massive ice-capped mountains of Kluane, largest and oldest of the Yukon's three national parks.

The Yukon's other two national parks, Ivvavik and Vuntut, are as far north of Kluane as you can go, and a world apart in the forces that have shaped them. The rounded mountains, rolling tundra and wetlands of these northern parks never were scoured by ice during the Pleistocene Epoch. Ivvavik, the northernmost of the two parks, protects an essential part of the migratory route of the Porcupine caribou herd.

Ivvavik is an Inuvialuit word meaning "a place for giving birth to and raising young, a nursery." Every year the 170,000 animals in the Porcupine caribou herd flow across this northern land like a tide. In the spring the caribou descend from the mountains to the coastal plain to bear their young. Later in summer, calves in tow, they ford the rivers of Ivvavik and clatter across the rocky ridges of the British Mountains.

These rounded, treeless peaks cover two-thirds of Ivvavik's 3,926 square miles (10,207 sq. km.). Polished by wind and water, the British Mountains are the only large mountain system in Canada that was completely unglaciated during the last Ice Age. The Malcolm, Babbage and Firth rivers carve their way through these mountains en route to the Beaufort Sea.

Grizzly bears roam throughout Ivvavik and polar bears use the coastal plain during winter. Muskoxen graze on the cottongrass tussocks of the coastal plain. Dall sheep are at the northern limit of their range in the British Mountains, and moose and wolves wander through the area. In late summer thousands of snow geese descend on the Firth River delta before migrating south. Golden eagles, rough-legged hawks, gyrfalcons and peregrine falcons nest in the mountains.

Most of the 150 or so people who visit Ivvavik every summer choose to raft down the whitewater canyons of the Firth River. From the river there are endless opportunities to wander the dry ridges of the British Mountains and watch for wildlife in the 24-hour daylight. The number of visitors remains small because getting to Ivvavik takes some

FACING PAGE: *Rafters inspect whitewater on the Firth River in Ivvavik National Park. The river is named for John Firth, Hudson's Bay Co. agent at Rampart House on the Porcupine River.* (Yukon Government)

First Nation members from northern Yukon hunt beluga whales from shore-based camps such as this along the Beaufort coast. (Laurent Dick)

commitment. Most people fly there from the town of Inuvik in the Northwest Territories, 124 miles (198 km.) to the east.

For all of its remoteness, Ivvavik has a long cultural history. The northern Yukon was home to the first people to enter the New World. The Inuvialuit and their ancestors have used this land for thousands of years. Along the Firth River, visitors can still see tent rings, circles of stones used to weigh down the edges of hide tents. Lines of boulders on the tundra were used to funnel caribou toward waiting hunters.

Today the Inuvialuit and the federal government together manage Ivvavik. When Ivvavik was established in 1984, it was the first national park in Canada created through a Native land claim settlement. Vuntut, its neighbor to the south, follows the same model, one which reflects the different attitude toward wilderness found in the Canadian North.

In both parks, Native people retain the right to continue a traditional way of life by hunting and trapping. Here protected areas are established to sustain both wildlife and Native cultures. Wilderness is not thought of as a place that is only open to transient visitors, but as a home for people who have used it for thousands of years.

Concerns about protecting the northern Yukon started not long after oil was discovered at Alaska's Prudhoe Bay in 1968. Major pipelines were soon proposed for the Canadian North, prompting an extensive series of public hearings into the possible impacts of these projects.

The Mackenzie Valley Pipeline Inquiry recommended against building any pipelines until Native land claims in the area were settled. The inquiry also opposed construction of any pipeline across the northern Yukon, suggesting instead that the area be set aside as a huge wilderness park and wildlife refuge.

This bold recommendation became a reality in 1995 when Vuntut was established through the land claim settlement of the Vuntut Gwitch'in First Nation. The park protects the northern portion of Old Crow Flats and the pediment hills rising above this wetland plain, a total area of 1,678 sq. miles (4,345 sq. km.).

Most of the southern portion of the flats is part of the Gwitch'in's land claim settlement area. Vuntut means "Crow Flats" in the Gwitch'in language, and this region has always been central to their culture. The maze of wetlands is also critical habitat for waterfowl.

In 1982, the flats were designated under an international convention as a Wetland of International Importance. The flats serve all major migratory flyways in North America, and the lakes and marshes there are considered exceptionally productive for an area 74 miles (118 km.) north of the Arctic Circle.

The Porcupine caribou herd migrates through Vuntut in fall, winter and spring, following the higher ground that rises above the flats. Together Vuntut and Ivvavik protect almost all of the herd's Canadian range, but the caribou's most critical habitat is still threatened. Energy companies want to open the coastal plain of the Arctic National Wildlife Refuge in Alaska to development. This area, known as the 1002 lands, is the herd's main calving ground.

Every summer paleontologists and archaeologists come to Old Crow Basin to look for remains of the Pleistocene mammals that took refuge here during the last Ice Age. Old Crow Basin is known as the richest paleontological and archaeological area in Canada, and paleontologists have dug thousands of fossils from the banks of the Old Crow River, which flows through the flats.

Just getting to Vuntut is an adventure, so distance and expense will limit the number of visitors to the park. The jumping off point, the Gwitch'in community of Old Crow, has no road access, so visitors must fly there and then arrange for local transportation into the park 40 miles (64 km.) to the north. A visitor reception center will be built in Old Crow, but there are no plans for facilities within the park.

There are two other protected areas in northern Yukon. Fishing Branch River, an ecological reserve, was also established through the Vuntut Gwitch'in land claim. A unique and vulnerable population of grizzly bears gathers on the river every fall to feed on a late run of chum salmon. The area is closed to hunting.

Herschel Island is the Yukon's first territorial park and only island. Located not

Unglaciated mountains flanking the Firth River are home to the northernmost populations of Dall sheep in the Yukon. Raptors such as gyrfalcons and golden eagles nest in the Firth River canyon. (Yukon Government)

The Richardson Mountains separate the Porcupine drainage and Eagle Plain in northern Yukon from the Mackenzie River valley to the east in the Northwest Territories. These mountains and the neighboring British Mountains to the west are the northernmost mountains on the Canadian mainland. (Laurent Dick)

far from the delta of the Firth River, Herschel was formed from sediments pushed up by ancient glaciers. This small plot of tundra measures only 44 square miles (114 sq. km.), but it has a rich natural and human heritage.

Aboriginal people have used Herschel as a fishing and hunting base for thousands of years. The island's population exploded in the 1880s when American whalers began hunting bowhead whales in the waters around Herschel. At one time, 1,500 people lived on the tiny island and the Royal Canadian Mounted Police maintained a post there until the 1960s.

In the summer, Herschel teems with life. Dozens of different species of birds have been spotted there. Both ringed and bearded seals can be seen in the surrounding waters, and from July to September, beluga and bowhead whales migrate past the island.

From Herschel, you travel the length of the territory to find the Yukon's other territorial park. Coal River Springs in southeast Yukon is ranked as one of Canada's most important thermal springs because of its extensive tufa formations. These delicate deposits of dissolved calcium are hidden in the forest just off the Coal River. The tufa formations cascade down the hillside in a series of terraces that are splashed with color in the summer. Bright yellow monkeyflowers encircle pools filled to the brim with aquamarine water; the smell of mint scents the air. The spring water is cool, not bubbling hot, but its steady temperature helps support the abundance of plant life. An ecological reserve was established here in 1990 to protect this miniature garden. No road access to this isolated site is planned because heavy visitor use would destroy the fragile tufa. Most visitors are boaters who have flown into the area to start their trips down the Coal River. However, determined visitors with fat pocketbooks could charter a helicopter from Watson Lake, 50 miles (80 km.) west of the springs.

It is a measure of the Yukon's wildness

BELOW LEFT: *Don Cornelius and daughter Mandy cross a rubble field of sedimentary rock in the North Ogilvie Mountains. The rubble field is one clue to the long period of weathering this region has undergone. Because this area is part of Beringia, relict populations of plants and animals, such as of a butterfly species whose females cannot fly, are found here. (Karen Cornelius)*

BELOW: *A cookpot hat makes a perfect foil for this persistent long-tailed jaeger. (Don Cornelius)*

ALASKA GEOGRAPHIC® 45

Rafters prepare for a journey down the Firth River in Ivvavik National Park and out onto the arctic plain to the Beaufort coast. Well-known Japanese musher and adventurer Jujiro Wada, and his partner Ben Smith, found gold in the Firth drainage in the first decade of the 20th century. In the years since, gold-seekers have continued the search, but viable payloads have yet to be found. (Leslie Kerr)

that Kluane is the only national or territorial park in the territory that is accessible by road. But the Yukon does offer the chance to drive one of the greatest wilderness adventure roads in the world. The Dempster Highway is one of only two public roads in North America that crosses the Arctic Circle. This two-lane strip of gravel stretches 460 miles (736 km.) from the Klondike Highway near Dawson City to Inuvik in the Northwest Territories. Along the way the Dempster traverses vast expanses of open tundra and two mountain ranges.

Along the southern end of the road, the jagged profile of Tombstone Mountain dominates the end of a long valley. This pinnacle is one of the Yukon's best-known and most cherished landmarks. A territorial park in the Tombstone area has been negotiated through the land claim of the Tr'on dek Hwech'in First Nation.

North of the Tombstones, in the Blackstone Uplands, the tundra stretches farther south than anywhere else in western Canada. This wide-open landscape provides endless opportunities for hiking and is a birder's paradise, offering one of the best opportunities in North America for observing birds of the Subarctic.

Not so long ago, the Yukon's rivers served as its highways. Today paddling down a northern river is one of the best ways to experience the territory. Four Yukon rivers have been either nominated or already designated as Canadian Heritage Rivers. They offer a small sampling of the spectacular river trips in this part of the world.

On the 30-Mile Section of the Yukon River, blue-green waters flow beneath steep bluffs and broad terraces. The wide, forested river valley is now a quiet wilderness but abandoned cabins and decaying paddlewheelers serve as haunting reminders of the Yukon's gold rush and riverboat heritage.

The Bonnet Plume, a heritage river nominee, descends swiftly through the Wernecke Mountains to the Peel River. Flowing through a wilderness of 12,350 square miles (32,110 sq. km.), the Bonnet Plume offers challenging whitewater and excellent alpine hiking. To paddlers, this is one of the premiere wilderness canoeing rivers on the continent.

The wild waters of the Yukon's other two heritage rivers run through one of the great wilderness areas of the world. Ribbons of green in a land of lofty peaks and immense glaciers, the Tatshenshini and the Alsek join together on their runs to the Pacific Ocean.

Highlight of the Coal River Springs Ecological Reserve in southeastern Yukon is this tufa formation above the Coal River. The river is part of the Mackenzie watershed, a 720,000-square-mile (1.8 million sq. km.) drainage basin for North America's largest north-flowing river. (Yukon Government)

The Tatshenshini, a heritage river candidate, swells in size as it races downstream, turning into a silt-laden, braided force. Salmon run against its powerful, icy waters and the tracks of bears and wolves line its sandbars.

The Yukon's first heritage river, the Alsek, has a starker, harsher beauty than does the Tatshenshini. From its headwaters in Kluane National Park, this river of rock and ice courses through old lava flows and an almost-unrunnable canyon. The Alsek and the Tatshenshini are the only rivers powerful enough to breach the barricade of the St. Elias Mountains.

The territory's newest protected area covers more placid waters. In the autumn as many as 10,000 ducks, geese and swans descend upon the Nisutlin River Delta National Wildlife Area to feed on its rich growth of aquatic plants. Located on Teslin Lake, the shallow waters of this protected bay provide important migratory waterfowl habitat for birds using the Pacific Flyway. Peregrine falcons also migrate through the area.

The Yukon is also a staging area for the most famous hike in the North, the Chilkoot Trail. This three- to five-day trip follows the

FACING PAGE: *Site of a wild camp during the heyday of arctic whaling, Point Simpson on Herschel Island saw the arrival of a missionary in 1896 and of a RNWMP detachment in 1903. Whaling and trading continued, although on a reduced scale, for several decades, but by the 1950s the settlement was mostly abandoned.* (Chlaus Lotscher)

ABOVE: *Vuntut Gwitch'in hunters cross Old Crow Flats, a portion of which lies within Vuntut National Park.* (Yukon Government)

route of the Klondike goldrushers, starting at tidewater in Alaska and crossing famous Chilkoot Pass. Heritage artifacts are still scattered along the 33-mile (53-km.) trail.

There are many different ways to experience this vast and varied land. Sea kayaking on the southern lakes has become increasingly popular. More people are mountain biking on the territory's quiet roads and trails. A few hardy visitors are discovering the attractions of the Yukon in its natural state of winter, exploring by dog sled, skis or snowshoes.

But the biggest draw remains the Yukon's wild nature and its healthy ecosystems. In the future the Yukon will have more lands set aside for conservation. Both the federal and territorial governments have committed to establishing protected areas in each of the Yukon's 23 distinct ecoregions. Almost all new protected areas will be established through Native land claim negotiations. ●

Precontact History

By Dr. Donald W. Clark

Editor's note: *Donald W. Clark studied at the University of Alaska Fairbanks and the University of Wisconsin-Madison, where he received his Ph.D. in anthropology. He retired from the position of curator of Yukon Archaeology and curator-in-charge of the Archaeological Survey of Canada, Canadian Museum of Civilization, in August 1997, and presently lives in Ottawa, Ontario. Dr. Clark has participated in or led nearly 40 digs in the District of Mackenzie, the Yukon, and along the Koyukuk River and around Kodiak Island in Alaska since the 1950s.*

Migration Era

Human history in the Yukon, as presently known, begins about 12,000 years ago, near the end of the last Ice Age. If humans occupied midcontinental regions of North America earlier, such colonizers also should have lived in the Yukon region, which lies astride the hypothesized route of early migrants from Asia. As the Ice Age was ending, most of southern and eastern Yukon remained icebound, but connections to the recently deglaciated east, and to the Mackenzie Valley in particular, were opening up through mountain valleys and along the arctic shore. With its low precipitation, the interior lowland had remained free of glaciers during the Ice Age. A broad, treeless landscape, known as Beringia, extended from western Yukon westward through Alaska and across Bering Strait to eastern Siberia. People became a part of the Beringian landscape late in its history. Thus far, the oldest evidence of human habitation from the Yukon comes from the Bluefish Cave rock shelters found not far south of Old Crow. Artifacts from this site are sparse because the small caves were not regular dwelling sites. At 12,000 to 13,000 years of age, some of the Bluefish stone tools indicate incursions of people with an Asian-derived microblade culture.

People of another early culture, called Nenana, were living in Alaska 12,500 years ago. Evidence of their existence has not been discovered in the Yukon, but a slightly younger occupation, the so-called Northern Cordilleran tradition, may be a late expression of the Nenana culture. Common Nenana tools that have survived in stone are end scrapers and side scraper bits, lanceolate points and heavy, rough tools, probably used for chopping. Northern Cordilleran sites are 10,000 to 11,000 years old and occur throughout the Yukon. Evidence of one division of the Northern Cordilleran tradition, the Flint Creek phase, has been found along the Firth River about 11 miles (17.6 km.) inland from the arctic coast. Flint Creek people hunted bison and caribou with spears tipped with small, lanceolate points.

FACING PAGE: *Excavators probe the gold-rush site of Canyon City, near Whitehorse, for clues to the lifestyle of early Europeans in the Yukon. Arrival of Westerners accelerated the changes influencing the lifestyles of the Yukon's First Nation peoples. (Heritage Branch, Tourism Yukon)*

LEFT: *This splitting adze may stem from A.D. 700 to 1000, a time period that seems to separate ancestral Dené people from earlier inhabitants of the Yukon. (Gabor Szilasi, Canadian Museum of Civilization, Ph.MiVO1:1)*

BELOW LEFT: *This selection of spear points, unearthed at the Klo-kut site, represents the work of ancestral Dené people. (Gabor Szilasi, Canadian Museum of Civilization,Ph. MjV1-1:1278)*

Also during this period late Paleo-Indians migrated north to the Yukon and Alaska. Evidence for their presence consists of fluted points found along a route leading from British Columbia and Alberta to the vicinity of Bering Strait. Possibly the Paleo-Indians and Northern Cordilleran people were closely related and amalgamated in the north. Just as possible, there were two early ethnic groups in the Yukon.

Microblade Technology Era

While Northern Cordilleran people were becoming established in the Yukon and Paleo-Indians were arriving from the south, new people, distinguished by their use of microblades, were coming into Alaska from Asia. Because little of this culture has survived other than stone artifacts, these people,

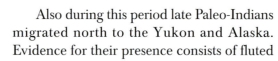

• Microblades •

Microblades are thin slivers of stone shaped like old injector razor blades. To obtain their consistent, flat, straight-sided shape, they were carefully produced from prepared cores of stone. At many campsites discarded, often flawed, microblades number into the hundreds and thousands. Yet the purpose of microblades remains poorly known. Uncommon finds of bone points in northern Europe, Siberia and western Alaska show that some microblades were inserted into grooves along the sides of arrow heads to produce a vicious weapon. In the Canadian Arctic, large microblades also were mounted at the end of elongate handles to make tools comparable to scalpels. A few specimens from the Yukon are heavily worn at the edges and clearly were tool blades. They would have worked well for tailoring skins for clothing and for cutting babiche strips (rawhide cord). But most microblades show no wear. Most are so delicate at 1/4 inch (.635 cm.) to as little as 1/10 inch (.254 cm.) in width that one is left wondering how these "spruce needle" microblades could have been used for anything. Perhaps there were not. Perhaps they were simply the play of ancient technicians demonstrating a peculiar expertise. •

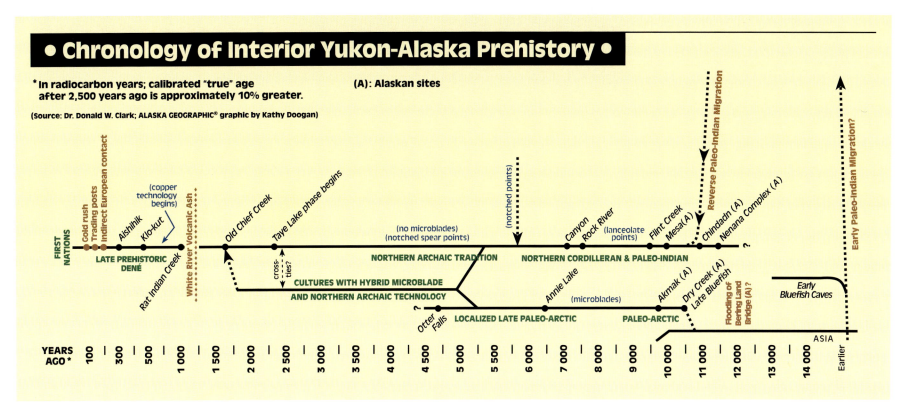

referred to as the Paleo-Arctic tradition, or Denali culture by archaeologists, are known mainly by their microblade industry though other tools, especially scrapers, lanceolate or leaf-shaped knives and spear points were used. These people first arrived in Alaska about 12,000 years ago and eventually spread into the Yukon. In some cases, it may have been the technology, not the people, that spread eastward. Later yet, perhaps only 6,000 years ago, the practice of using microblades was taken up across the mountains to the east in the District of Mackenzie, in the present-day Northwest Territories, and in northern Alberta to form the Northwest Microblade tradition of archaeologists.

Northern Archaic Times

Microblades continued to be made for several millennia, but during that time other aspects of ancient technology were changing. Most distinctive among these developments was the adoption, about 6,000 years ago, of short spear tips and knives that bore notches on their lower sides to facilitate hafting. The advent of notched points signals influence from the continent-wide archaic Indian cultures of the south and east, hence the broad designation "Northern Archaic tradition." At some localities in the Yukon, people ceased to use microblades, if they ever did, and other artifacts changed from styles of the microblade culture. This situation has given rise to hypotheses that either a new, archaic people migrated into the area from the south, or that the Northern Archaic tradition developed out of the Northern Cordilleran, bypassing the microblade culture. Elsewhere in the Yukon, though, notched spear points were simply added to the inventories of microblade-using people.

• An Ancient Skill Ensures Survival •

Ancient Yukoners relied on well-tanned hides for clothing to withstand winter temperatures as low as 70 F below zero (-59 C). To prepare hides for tanning, adhering flesh and fat were scraped off with an end-of-the-bone deflesher. If the hair was not to be left on, for warmth and appearance, the hides were depilated, either by cutting the hair off fresh hides or by scraping the hides part way through tanning after the hair was loosened. Skin under the hair was scraped off with a sharp beamer shaped like a drawknife. Then the hides were washed, dried and set aside to await an opportune time to continue the processing. At that time they were repeatedly soaked in a moose brains-water solution, wrung out, then laboriously worked with a tabular stone slab scraper that, among other things, imparted a suedelike finish to the leather. Other than the adoption of European tanning agents such as Lysol soap and experimentation with metal scraper bits and with churning hides in a washing machine, European technology could improve little on aboriginal methods for tanning skins. •

A staff member at the Gwitch'in Ancient Voices work camp near Dawson tans hides for use in the camp's traditional skills program. (Harry M. Walker)

Population continuity is seen in that instance, but with ongoing technological change. Details sometimes are unclear because of the variability in artifact inventories that has arisen through the vagaries of small samples and seasonal or functional differences between sites. Besides notched points and knives, people had generalized leaf-shaped spear tips; various types of stone scrapers to shape bone and wood, and to dress hides; stone knives; adzes that were used as axes; hand drills; net sinkers; barbed fish spears and thrusting lances. Few bone and antler tools have survived decay.

Later Peoples — Ancestral Dené

By 6,000 years ago ancient Yukoners had developed a way of life based on hunting and fishing that continued to historic times. Nevertheless, there were striking developments late in this period, especially the adoption of the bow and arrow and cold copper working, and the total demise of microblade use. Scientists recognize, thus, a late phase of cultural history to close out the scope of precontact development in the western Subarctic though its starting point is somewhat arbitrarily assigned. For the southern half of the Yukon, the White River volcanic ash dated at about A.D. 700 serves as a convenient time marker. The ash cloud spread out from a demolished volcano located in present-day Alaska, close to the southwest corner of the Yukon. This eruption undoubtedly snuffed out all life near the vent. Farther away, the ash fell in a blanket

5 inches to 8 inches (13 cm. to 20 cm.) thick in a linear zone that extended from a point southwest of Carmacks to the vicinity of Pelly Crossing, and in lesser depth far outside that zone. People would have been forced to leave the area for a year or two after the eruption and this would have disrupted their lives and those of neighboring bands, perhaps causing strife and starvation. The northern Yukon lacks such a field marker, but a comparable date, of about A.D. 700 to 1000, serves to divide later occupations by Dené (Northern Athabaskans) from those of their antecedents.

Stone tools from these ancestral Dené cultures include types known in earlier times, and also various adze bits, such as large, grooved splitting adze heads. By this period, ancient people fashioned tiny tips for various styles of arrowheads. At some late sites, scientists have found bone and antler artifacts that served as beamers and sewing awls, barbed arrowheads, bird and fish spear prongs, fish hooks, ornaments and other objects. Beamers are scrapers made of the leg bone, such as of the caribou, used to remove flesh from skins. Prior to introduction of steel skin-sewing needles with cutting edges at the tip, well-stitched, tailored clothes were made without needles because it is difficult to shove a conventional round needle through a tough hide. Instead, sinew was pushed through holes made with an awl. Food refuse shows what animals were hunted or trapped, with caribou, moose, hare and muskrat figuring prominently.

• A Northern Copper Age •

Subarctic people entered the metal age almost 1,000 years ago. Rather than use stone for many tools, a more precious material, native copper, was preferred when people could obtain it. Copper in its pure metallic state is found in the headwaters of the White River, near the Alaska border east of the Wrangell Mountains, and as nuggets in tributaries of the Copper River west of the Wrangells.

In addition to the locally obtained copper, western Alaskans had become familiar with iron, which was traded from Siberia in small pieces as early as A.D. 500, but there is no evidence that any of this iron reached the Yukon during prehistoric times.

The copper nuggets were hammered into thin sheets. Sheets then were trimmed and sharpened to make tools such as knife blades. For sturdier objects, a sheet was folded over on itself or small sheets were stacked and hammered to meld the layers together. If, in the process, the sheets became too brittle to fold without breaking, the copper was softened by heating, a process called annealing. This allowed relatively large tools, such as dagger-shaped knives, to be made of smaller pieces of copper. Small bars formed by folding were ground and bent into hooks, prongs, awls, ornaments and points. For arrowheads with long, narrow, pointed (rat-tailed) tangs, the blade of the point was left as a sheet (trimmed and sharpened), while the other portion was folded and refolded to build up the stem. ●

An obsidian flake and copper nuggets indicate early people adapted available raw materials for their use and traded with other groups. (Gabor Szilasi, Canadian Museum of Civilization, Ph. X1-B-179)

• Trade: An Essence of Humaness •

Sometimes ancient people traded to obtain better raw materials for tools and ornaments. Trade also allowed Native leaders to acquire goods that would enhance and maintain their status, items such as tusk-shaped dentalium shells, native copper for tools or prestigious foods to be presented to guests at feasts. Trade may have had its greatest appeal as a formalized meeting with peoples of other bands and tribes that offered opportunities for travel, dancing, sports contests, gaming, feasting and to renew old acquaintances. But sometimes the profit motive superseded these other goals, especially when groups that had little in common met. Then, trade could be what we might call "a rough diplomacy." If one group was weak and unwary, it often received little and might have its camp pillaged. Trade became raid. Archaeologists seek evidence of prehistoric trade for the clues that it provides of these very human of activities. Much that was traded was perishable and thus is missing from the record. But in ancient camp remains lie materials that have come far from their natural sources by being exchanged through middle men. A glassy fused rock (not obsidian) was used in the central Yukon near Carmacks. This stone originated near Fort Norman in the Mackenzie Valley. Obsidian (volcanic glass) was well-suited for projectile points and scrapers because it was easily flaked into sharp tools. Geologic sources located at Mount Edziza in British Columbia, near Kluane Lake in the Yukon and in Alaska all provided obsidian for early Yukon knappers. Native copper's presence at places distant from its origins flanking the Wrangell Mountains indicates that it, too, was a valuable item of trade. ●

This fish lure was found at the Klo-kut site. (Gabor Szilasi, Canadian Museum of Civilization, Ph. MjV1-1:66)

ABOVE: *This decorated beamer was found near Old Crow. (Gabor Szilasi, Canadian Museum of Civilization, Ph. MjV1-1:1531)*

FACING PAGE: *Selkirk First Nation students excavate a trench at Tatlmain Lake in the central Yukon. (Heritage Branch, Tourism Yukon)*

The Inuit Border

About 5,000 years ago Paleo-Eskimos swept eastward from Alaska across the narrow arctic coastal plain of the Yukon. Some stayed; others reached Greenland. These people are recognized by their specialized carving tool bits (burins) and exquisite, tiny flint artifacts. They are commonly referred to as the Arctic Small Tool tradition (ASTt). These people hunted caribou, muskoxen and elk. Undoubtedly they also hunted sea mammals along the coast, but their coastal campsites have been washed away. Instead, their remains come from such inland sites as Engigstciak on the Firth River.

Paleo-Eskimos of the Choris and Norton

cultures, which are best known from northwestern Alaska, continued to use Engigstciak from about 1,500 B.C. onward. Their tools were based on ASTt patterns, but with some additions and deletions. Among the additions was pottery, manifestation of a skill derived from Asia by way of Alaska.

For the last several centuries there have been Inupiat or Inuit villages along the northern Yukon coast and their hunters have ranged as far inland as the Old Crow Flats. "Inuit" is the self-name for most Arctic Eskimos north of Norton Sound on Alaska's Bering Sea coast, but Alaska Inuit, to whom northern Yukoners were closely related, distinguish themselves as Inupiat. Their ancient villages have been completely eroded away by the sea during the 20th century.

The Advent of Europeans

Beginning at the end of the 1700s and intensifying during early decades of the 1800s, Native Yukoners became the indirect recipients of European influence. This came from ship-based traders, from trading posts around Alaska and from posts located inland along the Mackenzie River in the present-day Northwest Territories. By 1850, the Hudson's Bay Co. had posts in the Yukon, though soon only Fort Yukon in Alaska, established in 1847, remained. But prior to the influx of prospectors at the end of the 1870s and the arrival of whalers on the Beaufort Sea, few Europeans lived in the Yukon. Initially, traders could only supplement Native lifeways. People still relied on hunting and fishing for subsistence and for the materials needed for construction and for winter clothing. But imported summer clothing, fabric for tentage, metal tools, kettles and baubles of the fur trade soon made a mark as significant additions to an ancient technology. ●

• Burins •

A burin is a slotting, gouging or scraping tool bit produced in a number of forms. Its defining characteristic is an edge produced and resharpened by a procedure in which, with one deft stroke, the toolmaker removes a flake or spall from along a margin or across the end of the stone tool. The edges of this facet then form the cutting edges of the tool. Some burins are nondescript bits of stone. The term also refers to a modern steel engraving tool. ●

FACING PAGE: *The Crow Flats have provided for the subsistence needs of the Yukon's people since precontact times. (Yukon Government)*

RIGHT: *This biface knife, flaked on both sides to the proper shape, was unearthed at Fort Selkirk and represents the Northern Archaic or ancestral Dené people. (Heritage Branch, Tourism Yukon)*

Sarah Abel of Old Crow

By Yvette Brend

Editor's note: *Yvette Brend was born in Seattle, and grew up in Victoria, British Columbia. A former reporter for the* Whitehorse Star, *she now works for the Canadian Broadcasting Corp.*

Sarah Abel sat in a Whitehorse hotel room in November 1997 sipping Orange Crush, with her Bible at her side. It was the third time in the 101-year-old Vuntut Gwitch'in woman's life she had left her home of Old Crow. The isolated village sits north of the Arctic Circle, about 620 (992 km.) miles north of Whitehorse. No roads go there. Abel's well-lined face grins when she tells stories about her home among the "good, fat" caribou, muskrats, moose and ripe blueberries. Of the three times she has left her village, twice were for medical treatment in the territorial capital, and once, for the death of her son, she took a trip to Inuvik in Canada's Northwest Territories.

There was never much need to leave Old Crow. The arctic wilds of the northern Yukon offered enough food and furs for the longtime trapper to feed and clothe her children after her husband died of tuberculosis more than 50 years ago. She flew south in 1997 in hopes the doctors could cure the cataracts clouding her eyes, but she left Whitehorse General Hospital disappointed. A lump growing behind an eye ruined her chances for the surgery that has allowed other elders to sew and bead once again.

Despite this, the woman born in Rampart House, a long-abandoned Hudson's Bay Co. trading post near the border with Alaska, grinned, perched on a hotel bed in her caribou and moose-hide-lined boots. She raved about the wonderful hospital, a far cry from the animal-skin tents where she remembers her brother was born. "The doctors and nurses they do good for me. Give me good grub," she said after a stay. Wild game confiscated from poachers by territorial conservation officers is often served to aboriginal patients. Despite clouded sight, Sarah still recalls a century of stories about the ebb and flow of ice jams, caribou herds and her people. Old Crow, originally a settlement of Loucheux Natives, got its name from a chief called Tetshim-Gevtik, meaning "Walking Crow." He died in the 1870s but left a strict code of high standards and moral principles. This code seems to be embodied in the teetotalling elder whose long hair is still kept in neat braids.

In the big city, Abel seems eclipsed by the world of machinery and fast food just outside her window. But her frailty conceals a strength that enabled this mother of 17 to support a family. She took the bad news about her vision well. After a century of life, she has seen worse setbacks, having buried

FACING PAGE: *Sara Abel was born at Rampart House, built as a Hudson's Bay Co. post on the Porcupine River after the company post at the junction of the Porcupine and Yukon rivers was closed. (Steve McCutcheon)*

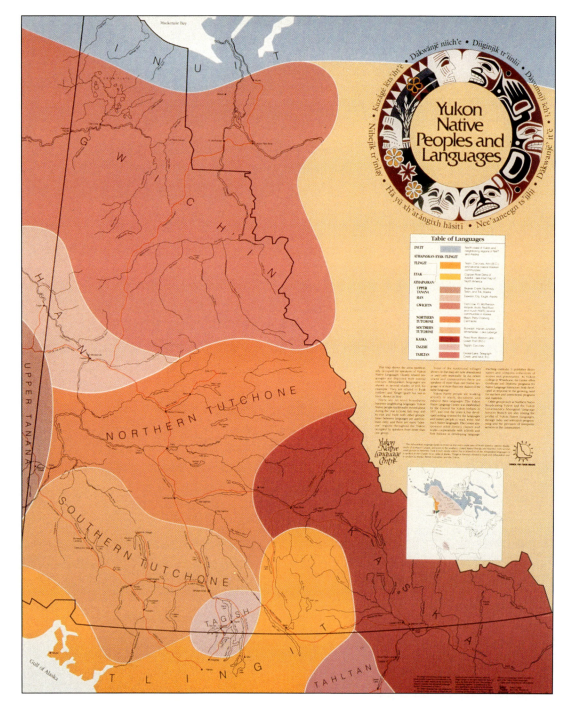

13 children and countless loved ones during those years.

Tuberculosis killed her 32-year-old husband when her youngest child was 11. After his death, she turned her hand to rifle, dog harness and trap, making her own boots and tanning her own hides. "She work just like a man," said Alfred Charlie, 74, who first met Sarah when he moved to Old Crow after growing up in the Bush, far from the community. "She do everything. She dry meat. She tan skins. She raise 17 kids. Her husband pass away on her and she had to make her living. She not marry again, you know, she look after herself real good." Charlie wed one of Sarah's nieces. He continued: "She train me to tan skin.... She's my grandma. She's a lot of kids' grandma."

Decades of work filled Sarah's head with tales of the wilderness. She often drove her dog sled alone, going off to collect firewood or check traps. "She's had 17 kids and she's still walking," said her granddaughter Lena Josie, 36, a receptionist at the Vuntut Gwitch'in First Nation office in Old Crow. Lena lived alongside her grandmother until the centenarian moved in with the youngest of her four surviving daughters in the summer of 1996. Lena misses her loving neighbor, who was always quick with hugs for her 15-year-old granddaughter Erica or with stories in their native tongue (formerly called Loucheux and now known as Gwitch'in) or with food for the ravens. The small-dog-sized, black birds are often referred to as crows despite the absence of crows this far north.

LEFT: *Dennis Frost of Old Crow replenishes his meat supply with this caribou. Caribou are a main food source for the Gwitch'in of the northern Yukon. (Yukon Government)*

ABOVE: *Sara Abel has seen a century of change come to her people, the Vuntut Gwitch'in of Old Crow. (Yvette Brend)*

"She always have prayers with us at night. She always fed the crows. She tells me one day I should take it over.... I feed them now."

Last year a near-fatal bout of pneumonia and heart problems forced Sarah to give up her own house beside her granddaughter and move into a spare room in a house with her youngest child, Annie Lord. She's not too demanding, but does not like "white man" food. Sarah still prefers caribou, dry meat or bannock, but she did try a hamburger on this visit to Whitehorse. She did not seem impressed.

"You have to have traditional food for her," said Annie, 63. "(Whitehorse) is too much for her now, but she used to trap, haul wood, tan skin and sew. She raised me up. She was both my mother and father. She worked just like a man." When Sarah got too weak to work, she turned to the church, helping out with the women's auxiliary of the St. Luke's Anglican Church of Old Crow.

Sarah also helped Order of Canada winner Edith Josie remember the lineage and history of her home village. Sarah's name appears regularly in "Here are the News," a column that ran for 30 years in the *Whitehorse Star* and eventually evolved into a book.

In February 1989, Edith wrote: "Too bad our parents and grandparents pass away so nobody tell us how relations go. But grandmother Sarah Abel tell Miss Josie...all the time. I was thankful for her to God and wish her good life and health."

Edith's wish came true. In April 1996, the *Whitehorse Star* noted the celebration of

ABOVE: *At home in the land of the Gwitch'in, Eliza Steamboat was 83 when this photo was taken in 1964. (Steve McCutcheon)*

RIGHT: *Photographer Steve McCutcheon speaks with Elisha Kwatlati, 87 when this photo was taken in 1964, who was chief of the Vuntut Gwitch'in at Old Crow for nearly two decades. The Chief holds two small northern pike. (Courtesy of Steve McCutcheon)*

Gwitch'in Kenneth Nukon explains his lifestyle to photographer Steve McCutcheon during McCutcheon's 1964 visit to Old Crow and the Porcupine River. (Courtesy of Steve McCutcheon)

Sarah's 100th birthday. "Sarah Abel is old but she still help herself and stay alone in her house. She was a small girl when her mother pass so old Peter Moses he took her and raise her, him and his wife Myra Moses.... Only four (of Sarah's) daughters living. They are Annie Lord, Dolly Josie, Marion D. Nukon and Eliza Martin (of Whitehorse)."

Sarah's sharp memories were also recorded in a book called *Rampart House* (1993) in which she recalls the Hudson's Bay post, and the surveyors burning log houses to rid the village of disease. She somehow survived the smallpox epidemic of 1911 that forced most Rampart House residents to resettle at Old Crow at the confluence of the Porcupine and Crow rivers.

Not surprisingly, Sarah has seen many changes since then. She remembers when the power came, the airport and the school. "That's how people lost their language," she said in 1993, often telling stories on CBC Radio in her native tongue, ever urging parents to teach their children the old ways and language. "She always talks about things we should do ... what's right and what's wrong and how to treat people," said granddaughter Lena, who has learned some of her grand-

mother's words in Gwitch'in and teaches them to her daughter Erica. "She's a very loving grandma. I miss living beside her. It's lonely now. I was with her all my life."

Sarah also knows such loneliness. She saw her son Charlie serve as chief and bring her community a school before he was taken by cancer. Since then, she has seen the deaths of sons, daughters and even an adopted grandson in an alcohol-related accident.

Sarah Abel is not known for taking any guff and often expressed concern about her community, which is officially "dry." Sarah never touches alcohol and throughout her life has often urged others to find a way to resolve recurrent drinking problems. "She was a very strong woman ... very strict. She always chased us home as kids," said Old Crow's current political representative, Robert Bruce, who admitted an alcohol problem caused his absence from the legislature during part of the last session and knows Sarah would not approve. "She kept people straight," he added. ●

FACING PAGE: *Subsistence flourishes among the Yukon's First Nation people where hunting, trapping, fishing and gathering supply a good share of their food and household needs. (Yukon Government)*

RIGHT: *Muskrat pelts are stretched to dry before being sewn into clothing at Old Crow. (Yukon Government)*

Yukon's Mining Industry

By John Steinbachs

Editor's note: *John Steinbachs is a former reporter who covered the mining beat for the* Whitehorse Star. *He now works for the Yukon Territorial Government.*

Several months ago, the mining economy of the Yukon was as bright as the sun on the summer afternoon I was hired by *Alaska Geographic®* to write this article. The task seemed simple. I had to write an article that illuminated the history and future of mining in the Yukon. The picture seemed rosy with new mines coming on line and hopes for the future bright. But the current state of the industry parallels that of earlier times: Boom and bust seems to characterize mining in the Yukon.

Gold

The mining industry in the territory began with a gold rush that attracted prospectors worldwide at the turn of the century. Then, almost as quickly as it began, the original Klondike gold rush was over. The volatility of those early days has left a permanent mark on the industry in the Yukon. Other, smaller rushes followed, always leaving ghost towns in their wake and a feeling of temporariness in every mining community.

In February 1997, BYG Natural Resources Ltd. was the perfect model of a small mining company on its way to becoming a successful player in the Yukon economy.

The company began limited operations at the Mount Nansen gold mine west of Carmacks and limited operations at the Ketza River mine, 186 miles (298 km.) away near Ross River. While they mined for ore, BYG used investor dollars to explore other properties like the Goddell Shear, a side of a mountain in southern Yukon. BYG also hoped to build a mill in Whitehorse that would service other mines in the territory.

The company's fortunes soured in October 1997 when a tailings pond at the Mount Nansen mine filled more quickly than expected because of the company's inability to effectively treat the water before discharging it into the environment. Faced with no alternative, the company laid off 60 employees in October. BYG reassured workers that the layoffs would only last six weeks or until the water treatment problem could be controlled, but as of early 1998, no workers had been called back. Even after the company solves the water problem, it will face a more frightening specter, low gold prices.

FACING PAGE: *Beginning in the mid-1800s, prospectors tested the gravels of hundreds of streams along the Yukon River looking for paying quantities of gold. They found enough color to generate rushes to the Stewart River and to the Fortymile. Not until 1896, when George Carmack, Skookum Jim and Tagish (Dawson) Charlie found bonanza in the Klondike Valley, did the Yukon gain worldwide fame as a gold-seekers dream. This view of the river shows the Yukon winding downstream from Dawson. (Danny Daniels)*

These low gold prices stem in part from the possibility that Switzerland and other countries might sell off much of their gold reserve, prompting some analysts to speculate that gold prices will drop to $250 per ounce. This possibility has generated fear in the industry. Miners and exploration geologists expected gold prices to hover around $380 an ounce at the end of 1997. Instead, prices dipped to $295 an ounce. For two years, the higher expectations and favorable metal prices prompted mining companies to raise exploration expenditures to record levels. In 1997, $57 million was spent on exploration in the Yukon, double the amount spent in 1993. No one will know until summer 1998 what effect the recent drop in world metal prices has had on the industry.

Many mines remain viable only if gold is priced at $250 an ounce or higher, explains Michael Attaway, vice president for operations at Viceroy Resources Ltd., which operates a mine in the Klondike drainage. His company has pre-sold its gold for the next two years and is safe, he says. But he is concerned for the exploration companies, placer miners and other gold companies that are facing low prices. These low prices are already forcing some placer miners to sell their claims and retire, and drilling to stop at many prospective gold properties.

Pioneer Mining

Placer miners have been hardest hit by the slump in gold prices. The downturn they are facing – almost unprecedented in the Yukon placer industry – is typical of the Yukon hardrock mining industry, whose boom-and-bust character is driven by international factors such as metal prices and exchange rates, or national and local policies such as investor confidence and taxation. But the desire for gold is relentless, and it was the same quest that brought thousands of people north during the Klondike gold rush.

In fact, the Klondike rush was created by three men on a creek in an unmapped area of western Yukon. On a sunny Aug. 17, 1896, George Carmack, Skookum Jim and Tagish (Dawson) Charlie were in the Klondike Valley chopping trees for rafts, fishing and doing a little prospecting. Earlier, Carmarck had met fellow prospector Robert (Bob) Henderson, who told them of a modest

No. 4 dredge lies anchored in the muck along Bonanza Creek Road outside of Dawson. When mining in the Klondike matured and conglomerates took over from individual miners and small companies, the conglomerates could afford to bring in big floating dredges to process the gravels more quickly. (Alissa Crandall)

A small dredge, abandoned when its crew left for World War I, rests along the shore of the Yukon River below Big Salmon. (Mike Doogan)

gold discovery along a creek in the Klondike drainage near what is now the town of Dawson City. By some accounts, Skookum Jim discovered the gold while looking for logs. Other accounts maintain George Carmack panned the nuggets. Regardless of who actually found the gold, that discovery sparked a rush that drew prospectors by the thousands, gold-seekers who combed the creeks draining into the Yukon River, then moved on to Alaska as new finds sparked repeated frenzies across the north.

The life of a miner at the turn of the 20th century was not easy, nor was reaching the Klondike. Well-to-do, would-be gold kings could hire passage on riverboats for a leisurely trip up the Yukon River from the port of St. Michael on the Bering Sea coast. Those in a hurry or short of funds had to hike over Chilkoot Pass or White Pass on trails from tidewater at Dyea or Skagway in Alaska, and travel down rivers or overland through forests to reach the Klondike. Once there, the stampeders found that the gold was not simply lying on the ground. Instead, they had to build fires, thaw the frozen gravel and dig shafts through 20 to 40 feet (6 to 12 m.) of permafrost to reach bedrock, near which lay the gold.

Since the discovery claim for the Klondike was staked in 1896, the gold-seekers who arrived in 1898 found most of the creeks in the Dawson area were already taken. Unable to find their own ground, these men and women either bought a claim or hired on to work existing claims.

Seemingly overnight, a tent city appeared at the junction of the Klondike and Yukon rivers. Dawson City was named for George Mercer Dawson, director of the Geological and Natural History Survey of Canada from 1895 to 1901. About 1887, Mercer had undertaken the first geological survey of Yukon Territory in association with William Ogilvie, Dominion land surveyor. Dawson City went from an area known for its good salmon fishing, to the site of a single trading post in August 1896, to the "Paris of the North," a city with restaurants, dance halls and an opera house by 1898.

As the number of miners in the Klondike Valley increased, so did gold production. In 1897, $2.5 million worth of gold was taken out of the ground. By 1900, that figure topped $22 million, when gold was worth only $20 an ounce.

Thirty thousand people roamed Dawson in its heyday. After 1900, the amount of gold being mined began to dwindle, and by 1921 the population of Dawson had dropped to

4,000, half of which were indigenous peoples.

About 800 placer miners still work the drainages that gave birth to the gold rush. In the year ending October 1997, these miners produced 109,000 ounces of gold for a gross value of $41 million.

Placer Mining Today

Art and Noreen Sailer head up one of the families of placer miners who started mining long after the Carmacks and Hendersons abandoned the Yukon. The Sailers move gravel on the banks of Dominion Creek, about 25 miles (40 km.) from George Carmack's discovery. Art explains that they first began gold panning on weekends in British Columbia. Back then, mining was more like a hobby for them. Fate delivered the two onto Quartz Creek in the Klondike during the 1960s, when the company Art worked for as a mechanic sent him to the Yukon to build a bridge.

Art and Noreen formed a partnership with another miner and began working a claim, equipped with an old bulldozer and a borrowed sluice box. The partnership continued with the Sailers working nights and weekends during the summer and moving back south again to work other construction projects in the winter.

FACING PAGE: *This view up Bonanza Creek in the Klondike Valley shows the heart of the Klondike gold rush. By 1900, more than $22 million in gold had come out of the Klondike area.* (David Rhode)

RIGHT: *At midcentury Dawson still retained its look of permanence, although its glory days during the Klondike gold rush had long passed. As the 20th century closes, tourism is generating renewed interest in Dawson, resulting in new shops and tourist outlets.* (Steve McCutcheon)

ABOVE RIGHT: *These engines ran to gold mines in the Dawson area at the turn of the century.* (Steve McCutcheon)

Gold claims mined in the 1890s in the Dawson area have been reworked profitably in the century following the gold rush. (Steve McCutcheon)

Every spring the couple returned to the Klondike to work their claim, and soon they had two youngsters in tow, children who now help run their operations on Dominion Creek. The gold-mining life offers a number of advantages, such as family-oriented living and wilderness, Art said. It does, however, have its down side. As he explained: They

A Geological Treasure Chest

The prospectors who initially came to the territory saw the potential for minerals other than gold. As they fanned out across the countryside, they stumbled onto silver, copper and zinc. The Yukon has such a rich mineral inventory because it is part of the Western Cordillera, a mountain chain running the length of the Western Hemisphere. Interaction of large tectonic plates that make up the earth's crust created this chain. When one plate moves under another plate, molten magma is formed and ascends into the upper plate where it cools to form granitic bodies called plutons. This input of heat drives the circulation of hot fluids within the crust that leads to the creation and concentration of metallic minerals in ore deposits.

"Things have to be happening to the rocks before you form mineral deposits," said Grant Abbott, acting chief geologist for the Yukon Geology Program. But for gold to concentrate in such magnitude to generate a rush the size of the Klondike stampede, another natural event had to bypass the Klondike.

During the Pleistocene Epoch, which ended roughly 10,000 years ago, glaciers covered much of northern North America. Since much of the Yukon and Alaska were in fact too dry to accumulate enough snow to make great continental glaciers, these areas, including the Klondike, escaped the glaciers excavating effects. As a result, the gravels that contain and had concentrated the gold were not bulldozed, smeared and disseminated throughout the region. The gold-bearing gravels had escaped glaciation and remained intact, waiting to be discovered by the prospectors. ●

A pronounced scar on the Klondike countryside exposes the White Channel Gravels, an ancient riverbed made up of pulverized talc and white quartz that is laced with gold. (Mike Doogan)

may not be digging for gold in smoky, frozen tunnels, but they still work hard. On Dominion Creek, 60- to 80-hour work-weeks are the norm, with the odd break to go into town. The family winters in Sooke, British Columbia, repairing equipment and planning for the next season.

Pondering the rolling, tree-covered hills, Art notes that there have been four generations of miners on Dominion Creek, and after each generation the trees and wildlife have returned. This is the beauty of placer mining to Art. No chemicals are used in the mining, so in effect all he and his crew are doing is moving dirt. Soon the yield will no longer be sufficient to make mining profitable with current technology and only some flakes of gold will be left to harvest. But with the ingenuity of people who hunt for gold, he is sure that new technology will make it profitable to collect the remaining flakes.

Other Metals

There are bright spots on the Yukon mining scene, like the proposed reopening of Cominco Ltd.'s Sa Dene Hes zinc mine

ABOVE LEFT: *The big mines that characterize the modern mining era tend to open and close with the fluctuation in metal prices and other economic factors. Today's Keno, a tiny settlement with a declining population, is the shadow of a former boomtown associated with Louis Bouvette's 1919 claim at a rich silver and galena deposit. The settlement, originally called Sheep Hill, took the name "Keno" after the gambling game.* (Steve McCutcheon)

LEFT: *Keno lies at the end of the Silver Trail, a road branching off the Klondike Highway between Whitehorse and Dawson at Stewart Crossing, running up the Stewart River valley to Mayo and on to Keno. The Guggenheims and Treadwell-Yukon Mining Co. opened up rich silver and lead ore deposits in the area that formed the basis for a thriving mining industry in the Stewart Valley.* (Yukon Government)

These trucks haul lead and zinc concentrate from the Anvil mine at Faro along the Klondike Highway to the seaport at Skagway, Alaska. (Steve McCutcheon)

outside of Watson Lake and the refinancing of the Faro lead and zinc mine owned by Anvil Range Mining Corp. Plans for a copper mine near Minto also continue. But metal prices have been down in recent months, which has diminished Cominco's enthusiasm for re-opening the Watson Lake mine. In late 1997 Cominco officials were saying that the summer 1998 start-up date may be pushed back pending better zinc prices.

These potentially economically viable deposits confirm that the Yukon is blessed with different types of minable metal resources. Lead, zinc, silver, copper, gold and tungsten deposits occur throughout the territory and provide great prospects for the future. But slumping metals prices and low investor confidence have slowed the rapid development of new mines that marked the past few years.

Development of these other metals has sustained the Yukon mining industry in years in which gold production has decreased. The production of silver began during the 1920s in the Keno Hill area of the Yukon, east of Dawson. A series of mines in the area, owned by United Keno Hill Mining Corp., became the world's fourth largest producer of silver. The mines eventually shut down in the 1980s,

FACING PAGE: *Elsa is the company town for United Keno Hill Mines, in its heyday one of the continent's largest silver producers. The mine closed in 1989 after a long run. (Steve McCutcheon)*

RIGHT: *Jim McLaughlin is mayor of the mining town of Faro. (Cathie Archbould)*

FAR RIGHT: *Lead and zinc is processed from the giant open pit mine at Faro. (Cathie Archbould)*

throwing hundreds out of work and leaving the community of Elsa a modern-day ghost town. United Keno has now formed a partnership with another company and may arrange the necessary funding to restart operations.

Another important discovery, this time of lead and zinc, occurred in the 1950s. Though not as glamorous as gold, lead and zinc from the Faro mine have produced more revenue than all the gold shipped out of the Yukon. More than 100 million tons of ore have been mined from three giant pits, and new plans by the company may take production underground. The mines have gone through a series of ownership changes and closures, spurring or slowing the Yukon economy with each change. Recently operations closed for eight months, restarting only after the company received a series of loans. As of late 1997, the mine employed about 1,000, directly or indirectly, a substantial impact when one considers that the Yukon's total population is 33,000.

Even those not employed by Anvil feel the effects of the mine's ups and downs. Anvil Range consumes 43 percent of the power produced by Yukon Energy Corp. When the mine goes down, power rates for other consumers increase significantly to help pay for the utility's infrastructure.

Anvil Range executives have said they are confident that more ore will be discovered on the company's claims near Faro. Even if Anvil is not able to find more ore, miners can look to the Ross River area where there are a few new large discoveries. The largest, Kudz Ze Kayah, is owned by Cominco. Next is the Wolverine, owned jointly by Westmin and Atna Resources. Both of these deposits benefit from being polymetallic, containing gold, silver, zinc, lead and copper. As a result, they avoid being dependent on the price of one metal and tend not be boom-and-bust mines.

Though the industry's future remains tenuous, there is no doubt the Yukon's economy needs the Faro mine and more mining development. With a little luck in the form of higher metal prices and more advancements in technology, that future could become more stable. ●

Pelly Pioneers at Ross River

By Norman E. Kagan

Editor's note: *Norman Kagan lives in Minnesota, but he grew up in New York City, and earned his first, second and third degrees in the sciences at Columbia, Stanford and the Rockefeller universities. For relaxation, he would lose himself on a wilderness river, none being better than the Ross and the Nahanni. After years of hearing the tall tales of that country, he decided to investigate, and has been most successful.*

The Ross River story has never been fully told. Of how a hardy breed of adventurous entrepreneurs began a community in the abundant southeast Yukon woodlands, drew others there with dreams of gold and sustained it with the fur trade. Official records, journals, letters, newspaper accounts and photographs reveal a glimpse of their lives.

Tom Smith, an American, perhaps the son of a black prospector from the Cassiar goldfields of British Columbia, had a prosperous fishing camp at Mica Creek (now Pelly Crossing), 50 miles (80 km.) up the Pelly from the Yukon River. The waters there teemed with whitefish from Tatlmain Lake, and demand for feed, both human and dog, was high. During his winter travels upriver, he found the Pelly rich in furs but lacking in supplies. Even tea and flour were wanting, and the few Natives he met were brewing leaves and digging for roots.

In the summer of 1901, Smith hired the shallow-bottomed steamer *Prospector* for the first powered trip up the Pelly, and moved his camp 200 miles (320 km.) upriver to its junction with the Ross River. The location was a backdoor into the Yukon, a natural crossroads for travelers coming north from the upper Liard River, or west over the mountains from the Mackenzie River. That winter, Smith built his trading post, and some 15 Native families settled nearby.

In 1902, Smith added to his stock with three visits by the new steamer *La France*. According to a *Dawson Daily News* feature story, on its second, mid-July trip, 46 passengers came along to see what all the fuss was about. The four women aboard noted the small rings of gold the Native women had in their nostrils. The men just noted the gold; some 30 of them (15 according to the *Whitehorse Star*) were prospectors with full-year outfits. Red Corning, Jack Stanier, Ira Van Bibber and Del Van Gorder were among these. Upstream from Smith's Landing, gold had been found on Ketza Creek, and J.J. Rutledge and J.M. Christie of Dawson were aboard representing a Dawson syndicate that had obtained rights to operate hydraulic mining there. And, Klondike co-discoverer

FACING PAGE: *In earlier years, by far the most common conveyance in the Yukon in summer was the riverboat, whether fancy river steamers or small skiffs. Hootalinqua, on the Teslin River west of the Ross River settlement, was an important stop for river traffic. Today remains of the river fleet can be found along riverbanks throughout the territory. (Mike Doogan)*

The Pelly Mountains offer this vista from the South Canol Road. The Pelly name comes from Robert Campbell's early expeditions to the area. Campbell named the Pelly River after Sir John Henry Pelly, governor of the Hudson's Bay Co. (Larry Anderson)

Bob Henderson was said to be sluicing placer gold in Hoole Canyon, whose rapids limited upstream navigation by riverboat.

As word of Smith's Landing spread, others settled there. Joe Coté, a French Canadian, built a rival trading post across the river on the Pelly's west side, opposite Smith's post and the mouth of the Ross River. Others built cabins on both sides of the river. In 1903, Fred Enevoldsen (later shortened to Envoldsen), a Dutch-American Klondiker who was a partner with Jim McDonald in the Dawson

Empire Hotel, so liked the country that he immediately returned to Dawson with the news of a wondrous gold strike, "a second Bonanza" wrote the *Daily News*. Enevoldsen rented the steamer *Wilbur Crimmins* for a stampede, and filled the vessel with his own supplies and paying, footloose prospectors. After a tedious trip upstream, the eager faithful, who had expected to kick up nuggets with their boots along the many river gravel bars, found little reward. The placer works that Henderson had at Hoole Canyon were deemed shallow and thin, and no one at Ross River had gold showings. Some stampeders wanted to tar and feather Enevoldsen, but most returned to Dawson on the *Crimmins*, disgruntled after only a few days. Ten did stay longer, insisting that Enevoldsen show them the Ketza River diggings. But they, too, soon returned to Dawson by raft, claiming that the "capricious" Enevoldsen had abandoned them. A week later, the Dutchman himself returned with Bob Henderson, whom he had gone ahead of the group to find. Henderson still felt the area had merit, but distanced himself from Enevoldsen.

Oliver Rose, a solitary man, settled at Blind Creek, 50 miles (80 km.) below Ross. His true name was LaRose. In late May of 1903, he was successfully running boats through Whitehorse Rapids, when a dear friend Lila Wallace persuaded him to take her through the rapids. Bud Harkin joined them. Their boat filled with water, and Lila leaned to one side, capsizing the boat. Only LaRose survived; Harkin left a widow with two small children. At Blind Creek, Rose ran a small post, and prospected and trapped over a wide range, but lived a desolate life in small hovels.

The ever-restless Tom Smith moved west in 1903 to Teslin Lake where he again saw conditions right for a trading post. He sold his Ross River post to Clement S. Lewis, who had arrived in August of 1902 on the third visit of the *La France*. Lewis was a well-educated young man, the second son of John Travers Lewis, the first Anglican Archbishop

Oliver LaRose, known as Rose, became a recluse at Blind Creek (shown here), on the Pelly River about 50 miles (80 km.) below Ross River. LaRose had been a successful river pilot at Whitehorse when a boat under his responsibility overturned and two people drowned in 1903. LaRose left Whitehorse, changed his name and operated the tiny post at Blind Creek when he wasn't prospecting or trapping. LaRose was committed to an asylum in 1925. (Photo 90/19 #40, Back Collection, Yukon Archives, courtesy of Norman Kagan)

of Ontario. On hearing of the Klondike strike in 1897, young Lewis had left Trinity College to see the area for himself. Steaming up the Yukon from its delta near St. Michael, Alaska, he toured the country and returned home with the latest news. But he couldn't settle back into his studies. In 1898, he returned north to Skagway, crossed Chilkoot Pass and headed for the goldfields. Later, he joined the stampede to Nome and Tanana. But the upper Pelly held his interest, and here he stayed. His father, the Archbishop, had died in 1901, leaving Lewis a small inheritance.

Teslin Lake began to draw attention in 1905 as rumors of gold strikes there hit the newspapers. Tom Smith bought the steamer *Quick* that spring, built barges and began moving freight and passengers twice weekly up the Hootalinqua (Teslin) River to Teslin. In October, he sold his new fur post to the expanding Whitehorse trading firm of Isaac Taylor and William Drury, and John Drury, Bill's brother, took charge. Tom Smith, with his partners Capt. A.F. Daughtry and Eng. George Waltenberg, enlarged the *Quick* for greater service in 1906. But troubles arose in 1907, though Smith managed to keep ahead of them. The T&D post burned to the ground in February, but its stock was saved and a new post was built. In June of 1907, Tom sold his interest in the *Quick* to his partners, and launched a new steamer, the *Frontiersman*, in August. At that same time, the *Quick* blew a cylinder, and Captain Daughtry, unable to pay the crew's wages, disappeared, later writing a letter of explanation from Vancouver.

Poole Field arrived at Ross River by 1903, perhaps with Clement Lewis. Field had come into the Yukon as a North West Mounted Police recruit skilled in the handling of horses and dogs. He was 17 when he joined the force at Regina, Saskatchewan, in June 1898, and immediately requested Yukon service. Sent north with a special detachment of Labrador dogs in November, he served a two-year assignment at the Tagish Customs Post, then took his discharge. He spent the next years in Alaska, where he mushed the winter mail between Nome and St. Michael, and explored the Tanana River above Fairbanks, then returned to the Yukon. Field had a unique perspective because he had received a legacy handed down to him by Robert Campbell, the first European Pelly River pioneer and a family friend.

These travelers begin the portage of Hoole Canyon on the Pelly River in the 1920s. (Photo 7665, Claude Tidd Collection, Yukon Archives, courtesy of Norman Kagan)

Campbell was recruited in Scotland by the Hudson's Bay Co. (HBC) when he was 22, and brought to Fort Garry, today's Winnipeg, in 1830 to help manage a new experimental farm on the Assiniboine River. He gained renown among horse racing fans by caring for Fireaway, an English thoroughbred brought to Canada to improve local stock. But Campbell wanted to be an explorer regardless of the hardships. In 1834, he was sent to

A Northwest Mounted Police Station weathers away at Hootalinqua where the Teslin and Yukon rivers meet. This location was the end of the Stikine Trail, which begins at Wrangell in southeastern Alaska. (Mike Doogan)

Another important settlement on the river corridors of the Yukon was Fort Selkirk, originally a Robert-Campbell-founded Hudson's Bay Co. post at the junction of the Pelly and Yukon rivers. (George Wuerthner)

Fort Simpson at the junction of the Liard and Mackenzie rivers. The HBC handed him the thankless task of extending its trade route up the perilous Liard into the interior of the Yukon. It was not a profitable route, but for years the company had sought the lucrative Pacific coast fur trade that the Russians enjoyed with the coastal Tlingit Indians, and it helped the negotiations if the Russians and the Tlingits thought that their monopoly of interior trade was at risk. Once the coastal concessions were obtained, the HBC did not object to the Tlingits pushing Campbell out of Fort Selkirk, which he established at the junction of the Pelly and Yukon rivers in 1852, and the HBC never permitted him to return. He continued to serve the company for another 18 years, but was dismissed from his chief trader position for a minor infraction of company rules in 1871.

After his Yukon days, Campbell returned to the Assiniboine in western Manitoba and renewed an old friendship with Allan McIver, another former HBC servant, Scotsman and horse racing enthusiast. McIver had married Elizabeth Beads, the Iroquois Metis daughter of John Beads, another HBC servant. Elizabeth's brothers were highly esteemed scouts for Dr. John Rae and John Paliser, and Elizabeth's own daughter, Catherine McIver, had married McIver's business partner, Edward Field, Poole Field's father. The Field family had a noble British lineage going back to the 14th century. Sir Frederick Laurie Field, a cousin, would rise to the highest rank in the Admiralty, Lord of the Seas. But Edward Field's family fortunes had fallen, and he emigrated to the Red River settlement to start a new life. After joining with Allan McIver in a Red River cart transporting business, Edward Field became a merchant, land developer, justice of the peace and the founding father of Wadena, Saskatchewan, where Poole Field grew up. As a child, Poole Field heard, perhaps firsthand, the tales of Yukon exploration by Robert Campbell.

Campbell had been sent up the Liard River, around the infamous Rapids of the Drowned in the Liard Grand Canyon, to the abandoned Fort Halkett post at the mouth of the Smith River in present-day British Columbia. From there, he scouted up the Dease River into British Columbia and up the Frances River into the Yukon, making contact with the interior Indians. In the Yukon, he established posts at Frances Lake, Pelly Banks at the Liard-Pelly divide, and at the mouth of the Pelly (Fort Selkirk). Were it not for the intervention of the nomadic Nahanni Indians, who were led by a chieftainess, he and his men might have been murdered or have starved to death. Campbell's ultimate triumph was the 1851 discovery of the true nature of the Pelly, when he and his men traveled downriver and arrived at Fort Yukon, a HBC post at the mouth of the Porcupine River in present-day Alaska. From there he traveled northeast to Fort MacPherson and the Mackenzie River, then upriver to Fort Simpson. Campbell had circumnavigated the whole of the Mackenzie Mountains. Yet the following year he was expelled from the land he discovered.

At Ross River, Poole Field mingled easily with both white and Native populations. He and Lewis established a camp up the Ross River at three small lakes that were named Lewis, Field and Rudyard. The fortress-like mountain above they called Kipling Mountain. Both men admired the works of Rudyard Kipling and Lewis had all of his books in his cabin library. (Rudyard Lake and Kipling Mountain are now called Sheldon lake and mountain.) Farther upriver at the Yukon-Northwest Territories border, Natives from both sides would winter and trap, and

Log buildings still serve as useful dwellings in Ross River. (Steve McCutcheon)

A healer and traveler known to some as Little Doctor, this man ranged throughout Ross River country. He died of old age at McEvoy Lake near the Pelly headwaters in the 1930s. This photo was taken about 1924. (Photo 7116, Claude Tidd Collection, Yukon Archives, courtesy of Norman Kagan)

here Field met the Natives from Fort Norman on the Mackenzie River. About 1905, he joined them on their migration over the mountains, down the Nahanni and Mackenzie rivers to Fort Norman and up the Great Bear River to Great Bear Lake and back again. In the meantime, Lewis sold their post, which they had named Nahanni House, to Taylor and Drury and stayed on to work for them.

In the summer of 1906, Fred Enevoldsen and his wife, Mary, returned to their settlement a quarter mile (.4 km.) below Hoole Canyon. Enevoldsen had left the upper Pelly after two years of prospecting and trapping to return to his former position as a contractor for the U.S. Army in San Francisco in 1905. But that came to an abrupt end with the 1906 earthquake. For the next 10 years, they again lived on the upper Pelly. Mary, as the only white woman in the region, garnered much attention. Often she was alone, but she was as capable as any man and on good terms with the Indians who visited her. She would share her garden produce and treat their illnesses, and gained a reputation as a healer. One chief took particular note of her skills.

He later came to be called "Little Doctor" because he would administer to other Indians. As a youth, he had met Robert Campbell at Pelly Banks, and during his long life, Little Doctor often retold stories of those days.

By 1908, Field was again at Ross River with his Native wife, Kittie Tom, who was pregnant. That summer they traveled downriver to Dawson where they married in St. David's Anglican Church. Field also reported to Capt. Fitz Horrigan of the Royal Northwest Mounted Police that the Ross River Indians were feuding with a group at Blind Creek. Pelly Indian Liard Bob had killed Blind Creek Jonathan, and Jonathan's brother, Ijutth, chief of the Blind Creek band, sought revenge. Horrigan arrived in the area to negotiate a truce, and Poole Field rose in local esteem. As interpreter and middleman, Field was able to trade furs between the Natives and Clement Lewis or Joe Coté to his advantage. His influence had other merits. With Del Van Gorder, Field established his own trading post, but the ever-fluctuating price of furs caught them off guard, and they later had to claim a loss due to "theft," perhaps to avoid repayment to their creditors.

Ross River continued to grow as a supply and fur center, and more Mackenzie River and Liard River Indians visited the post. Poole Field was responsible for this new eastern trade. He was a natural leader, a gifted storyteller and fluent in several languages. He praised the riches of the Yukon, the advantages of not trading with the Hudson's Bay Co., which held a virtual monopoly across the

Sometimes partners, sometimes competitors, Billy Atkinson and Poole Field spearheaded many of the efforts to open Pelly River country. Here the two families gather in 1914 in the field behind the Taylor and Drury post at Ross River. Back row are Billy Atkinson (left) and Poole Field; front row are the Atkinson boy, Mary Atkinson, Tannie Field, Kittie Field and the Fields' younger daughter. (Photo 8582, C. Swanson Collection, Yukon Archives, courtesy of Norman Kagan)

mountains in the Northwest Territories, and enticed others to visit his Nahanni House trading post.

William Atkinson came into the territory in 1911. He was a big man with a drooping shoulder due to a bullet wound that some say was acquired in a saloon fight. His Cree Metis family had supported Louis Riel and the 1885 Rebellion. With him was his young second wife, Mary Laferte. Mary, born Marie Adele Lanoix in 1884 at Fort Resolution, married Atkinson on Feb. 7, 1902, at Fort Providence, Northwest Territories. Field and Ira Van Bibber had met them on the South Nahanni River in the Northwest Territories. Atkinson was about 10 years older than Field, and a skilled traveler and fiddle player. He took readily to the Yukon and transporting goods along its rivers and trails. The team of Field and Atkinson was formidable, and even William Drury, who visited his company's post several times a year, made concessions to them.

In 1912, Clem Lewis left Ross River to take charge of the Teslin Lake Taylor and Drury post. Roy Buttle eventually ran the Ross River operation for Taylor and Drury. Though Lewis left his fine library behind, at Teslin Lake a greater prize awaited him. On a visit with Tom Smith, who had opened a rival post and married at Teslin, Lewis became reacquainted with Angela Ward, 16, whom he had met in 1898 in Skagway. According to the Lewis family, Clem had been in Skagway when the bullets flew

between Jefferson "Soapy" Smith and Frank Reid. Also there on the street was a two-year-old girl that had wandered away from her mother. Lewis drew the girl to him and they both hid behind some barrels during the gunfight. To quiet the girl, Lewis had given her a shiny gold nugget he had from his first Yukon visit. Angela still had that nugget 14 years later. In 1912, they married, and their first child, Iris, born a year later, they nicknamed "Nugget." In 1914, the Lewis family moved to a new post on the Liard River, near present-day Watson Lake, and continued to prosper.

The Ross River community also drew the attention of the Anglican church. Bishop I.O. Stringer wanted a presence on the Pelly and, in 1913, he recruited Cecil Swanson, a novice deacon. With his wife, Enid, they built a mission at Little Salmon and ministered from Carmacks to Hoole Canyon. In August 1914, they traveled to Ross River where a large gathering of Indians occurred yearly. In his memoirs, Swanson wrote: "I loved that wilderness country at Ross River. One year I estimated that close to 1,100 Indians gathered there in the summer. There were visitors from Yukon, Pelly, Liard, Fort Norman, Mackenzie, and a family from Stewart, British Columbia." Throughout his visit, Poole Field stayed by his side, interpreting and assisting with the services and classes. Also there was Dr. James Omar Lachapelle of Dawson. Lachapelle was the last of four doctors who had come into the country with the gold rush. He knew the limitations of his medications and supplies, but his comparative indifference toward the Natives' ills, at least in Swanson's eyes, disturbed the young deacon. Swanson made an extra effort to attend to their needs, while criticizing the good doctor in letters to the bishop. In 1915, Swanson was reassigned to the Whitehorse mission, and in 1917 he left, but he never forgot his Yukon experience.

For Poole Field these were glory years. His influence had grown, and his reach extended even to Ottawa. Following the example of Clem Lewis, who was gathering Native artifacts at Teslin Lake for the Museum of Canada, Field wrote to the head of the Geographical Service of Canada. He sent them items of interest, now kept at the Museum of Civilization, and the first of several letters describing the history and beliefs of the Mountain Indians with whom he traveled.

By 1917, the war in Europe dominated the outside news. Fred Enevoldsen couldn't remain in seclusion. He enlisted in a northern British Columbia forestry brigade and was sent to France. Mary, his wife, remained,

FACING PAGE: *The Ross River community gathers at the Taylor and Drury post in 1914. Bill Drury is the tall, hatless man in suit at left center. The Atkinsons are at center, Mary standing and wearing a straw hat, Billy sitting. Next to them at right are Kittie Field standing and Poole Field sitting. (Photo 6951, W. Hare Collection, Yukon Archives, courtesy of Norman Kagan)*

RIGHT: *Deacon Cecil Swanson (left) and his wife, Enid, (sitting) share a social call with Bishop and Mrs. Stringer and their children at the Little Salmon Anglican Mission in 1914. (Photo 8580, C. Swanson Collection, Yukon Archives, courtesy of Norman Kagan)*

splitting her time between Dawson and Hoole Canyon. Unlike Enevoldsen, however, Yukoners of German descent felt differently. Paul Fritz Guder had dreamed of the Yukon as a young lad in Silesia. By his 18th birthday, in 1912, he had arrived, and he had no wish to return. But Canadian authorities were suspicious of the newcomer. They detained Guder in Dawson, and took his guns away. After his release, he heeded the good advice of Poole Field and headed for a life of adventure on the Pelly where his nationality was of little consequence. A quiet, self-reliant man, he gained the respect of others and helped some such as Tom Bee and Billy Langham to find wealth in the mountains.

Tom Bee had served five years in the NWMP, and took his discharge in 1907 to join the American civil war veteran Capt. Henry Seymour Back of Carmacks in a prospecting venture on Nansen Creek. It was a harsh life. Bee lost both his big toes to frostbite in 1910, but he and Back's son Frank did find a discovery claim that year. After a trip home to England in 1912 (he returned on the *Lusitania*, leaving two days after the *Titanic* had sailed), he settled at Carmacks. Taylor and Drury had bought the Shaw and Rowlinson trading post there, and Bee joined Shaw to learn the business. He soon took charge of the post and began sending supplies by horseback to his friends on Nansen Creek. By the following year, Bee had opened his own post at Carmacks, and had married the visiting daughter of his patron, Captain Back. In 1914, Bee expanded his trading range to Ross River, perhaps by buying an interest in Joe Coté's post.

But troubling days soon visited Ross River. Field's wife, Kittie, came down with pneumonia and died in Hoole Canyon where she was buried. Field's younger daughter and Atkinson's son also died. And because Atkinson was often away, after a time Field and Mary Atkinson found comfort in each other's company. It is said that when Atkinson returned one day and learned of his loss, he wanted to cross the river and kill them both, but cooler heads prevailed. Field and Mary left for Dawson; Billy Atkinson subsequently had two more wives, two sons and grandchildren.

Tom Bee's post was never the same. Some say the doors had been left open and all the goods were taken. When Bee arrived with his wife and 3-year-old son, Austin, at Ross River in July 1917, there certainly was some trouble because Bee immediately placed his family in the care of Joe Winterholt and two Indian boys and set them off down the Pelly in a moosehide boat, taking with them the winter's valuable furs. The Rev. Cecil Swanson just happened to be aboard the steamer *White Horse* at the mouth of the Pelly when they met Mrs. Bee's party. The skiff had struck a rock and tore a hole in its moosehide skin that was temporarily plugged with a sweater. When the smaller boat attempted to come alongside the *White Horse*, their boat was swept under the steamer's counter, the wide, flat ledge at the first level deck extending beyond the hull. After some excitement, Mrs. Bee and her boy were hoisted to safety. "The incident ended safely for all concerned, but while it lasted, it was dangerous in the extreme," stated Swanson to the *Whitehorse Star*.

Field, his older daughter, Tannie, and Mary stayed in the Yukon for an additional

Angela Ward Lewis poses with her children in 1919. Her daughter, Iris, known as Nugget, holds the doll. (From Iris Lewis Hamilton, courtesy of Norman Kagan)

Fritz Guder and his dog, Teddy, pose near their Ross River camp about 1919. (Photo 90/19 #284, Back Collection, Yukon Archives, courtesy of Norman Kagan)

two years, mostly at Carmacks. Then they traveled by coastal steamer out of Skagway to Vancouver, and by train through Edmonton to the Athabasca waterway. With Jujiro Wada, the famous arctic musher of Japanese descent, whom Field knew from his Tanana days, they shared a Northern Traders river scow down the Mackenzie River to Fort Simpson. Wada continued on to trade along the arctic coast, and the Fields headed up the Liard to the South Nahanni. After a time, Joe Coté, Jack Stanier and other Yukon friends joined them, and again Poole Field's fortunes rose.

Fritz Guder remained at Ross River, and helped Tom Bee. On his own, Guder crossed from the Ross Valley into the Nahanni in 1919 to explore. And by word of mouth, Field lured Tom Smith, Frank Rae, Afe Brown and Bill Langham for a Nahanni prospecting trip in 1921. But the heady days at Ross River had passed. A severe drought in the summer of 1920 led to forest fires that raged for 160 miles (256 km.) on both sides of the Pelly from 40 miles (64 km.) above the Macmillan River to the Ross River. Dr. Lachapelle and Indian agent John Hawksley got through on the steamer *Thistle* and found the entire summer community of some 200 Indians and whites had been fighting the blaze for two days on both sides of the river. Both trading posts had been saved. However, that summer oil was discovered below Fort Norman in the Northwest Territories. Soon independent traders began to establish new posts there, and by 1921, the Indians who had gathered around Ross River began to return to the Northwest Territories side.

In a last burst of enthusiasm that winter Tom Bee, Fritz Guder, Frank Etzel, Joe Ladue and others stampeded over the Selwyn and Mackenzie mountains, mushing up the old Fort Norman Indian trail to the oilfields in 22 days. There they staked claims and returned quickly to the Yukon and on to Edmonton by way of Skagway to file the claims. Afterwards,

LEFT: *After a hunt in 1914, from left, Bill Drury, Dr. LaChapelle from Dawson and Tom Bee show off their duck kill at Carmacks. (Photo 90/19 #35, Back Collection, Yukon Archives, courtesy of Norman Kagan)*

FACING PAGE: *The Klondike Highway crosses the Pelly River at Pelly Crossing, about half way between Whitehorse and Dawson. (George Wuerthner)*

Bee left the Yukon with his family, returning briefly some years later to work a claim with Guder and Langham on Mount Freegold, 30 miles (48 km.) northwest of Carmacks. Old man Rose, the Pelly recluse, tried to hang himself in 1925 and was taken to an asylum. Clem Lewis closed the Liard Post in 1919 and took his family to northern British Columbia and later to southern Alberta where they lived a long life. Del Van Gorder operated a new post for Taylor and Drury at Pelly Banks, and his friend Ira Van Bibber raised a family of 15 children at Tom Smith's old fishing camp, now called Pelly Crossing.

Tom Smith continued to trap in the southern Yukon. His Indian wife died at Teslin in 1914, leaving him with a daughter, Jane, and two small boys. In 1926, concerned with leaving his teenage daughter alone, he took Jane along to his Liard Hot Springs trapping camp. The following spring they attempted to raft through the Liard's lower canyon and upset in the Rapids of the Drowned. Smith vanished, but Jane managed to reach land. She was rescued and taken to the Catholic mission at Fort Simpson. Nineteen months later, she gave birth to a boy and later moved to Hay River where she died of pneumonia in 1932.

William Drury continued to travel for many years throughout the Yukon, tending to his many posts. Dr. Lachapelle disappeared somewhere below Mayo while on an autumn hunt up the Stewart River. Only his overturned boat was recovered. Little Doctor had many grandchildren and lived to be 100. Fred Enevoldsen returned to the Pelly after the war, owned a river steamer, *The Veteran*, and numerous mining claims, was librarian in Dawson and remained active well into his 90s.

Field continued to trade and promote the Nahanni from the Northwest Territories side. He and Mary Atkinson Field raised two children of their own. In 1945, with the assistance of Fred Enevoldsen who drew in new backers, Field took his family north to the Yukon's Firth River where his friend Jujiro Wada had found gold. The gold was still there, but only commercially viable by hydraulic mining. In 1948, Field fell ill with cancer and was taken to St. Paul's Hospital in Vancouver where he died on April 22. As it happened, the Rev. Cecil Swanson was at Christ Church Cathedral in Vancouver, and he officiated at Field's burial in the Forest Lawn Cemetery, stating that of all the men of the North that he was privileged to meet, Poole Field was one of the finest, and "the best musher he had ever known."

Fate still held some twists for the Field family. Mary moved back to Dawson and

found work at the Senior's Home. Her former husband, Billy, who was retired and living at Teslin, developed a gangrenous big toe that he tried to remove himself. That brought him to the Dawson Senior's Home too, where he remained until his death in 1955. He played his fiddle and entertained until his dying days, but Mary never enjoyed his tunes.

In an oversight, a marker was never set upon Poole Field's Forest Lawn grave. A monument will be laid there in November 1998, 50 years after his death and 100 after he first passed through Vancouver on his way north. ●

FACING PAGE: *The Nahanni Range Road crosses the Frances River in southeastern Yukon. This road and the North Canol Road are the only two vehicle routes through the Selwyn and Logan mountains from the Yukon's interior to the Northwest Territories border, areas that the Pelly River pioneers traversed. (Larry Anderson)*

ABOVE RIGHT: *The Taylor and Drury trading post stood on the east side of the Pelly River at the mouth of Ross River in 1942. (Photo 89/35 #2, W. Phelps Collection, Yukon Archives, courtesy of Norman Kagan)*

RIGHT: *A fence marks Joe Cote's trading post on the west side of the Pelly River opposite the mouth of Ross River. (Photo 89/41 Album 5 #875m Anglican Church Collection, Yukon Archives, courtesy of Norman Kagan)*

The Yukon In Celluloid

By Frank Norris

Editor's note: *Frank Norris is a National Park Service historian living in Anchorage. He is co-author of* Chilkoot Trail, Heritage Route to the Klondike *(1996).*

Novelist Walker Percy has noted that a place becomes real only when perceived on the silver screen. If this is true, then the Yukon is a frozen frontier populated by prospectors, outlaws, sled dogs, stout-hearted Mounted Policemen, dance-hall women and other hard-bitten characters on the fringes of life. Hollywood, in its search for a good story, has found the north country too exciting to ignore; more than 100 feature-length films have been produced about the Yukon. Such an impressive output, of course, had a major impact on the public's perception of the Yukon, particularly between 1910 and the 1950s. But why did Hollywood perceive the North as it did? And how have those images changed over the years?

Prior to the 1890s, the outside world knew next to nothing about either Alaska or the Canadian northwest. But in July 1897, Alaska and the Yukon became household words, and for the next year or so the gold rush was front page news. As a result, the region became known for its gold resources and little else. The rush also tended to fuse the images of Alaska and the Yukon together.

The Klondike rush brought forth the first popular literature about the north country. First came a flood of guidebooks describing the land, then travel accounts appeared in hometown newspapers. Soon afterward came the dime novels and similar pulp fiction; publishers cranked out more than 100 of them with a gold rush theme.

Before long, more sophisticated literature began to emerge. Jack London, an unknown Californian, trekked north in July 1897. Using the animal story, a popular literary genre, London wrote *The Call of the Wild* (1903) and *White Fang* (1906). Both books were successful, in part, because of the way he portrayed the North: a pitiless, icebound landscape where any sign of life was an affront.

About 1910 a new art form, the motion picture, became popular. Before long, the first one-reelers were being released about the north country, bearing such titles as "Code of the Yukon," "Justice in the Far North," "Kid from the Klondike" and "North of 53." Most dealt with the Klondike rush. Authenticity was not their strong suit; a 1912 Selig production, called "The Ace of Spades," has been described as "a 'Klondike' picture in which the gold fields were set in the American southwest."

As motion pictures matured, feature-length productions became the norm. Audiences of the day had learned about the

FACING PAGE: *More than 100 feature-length films have been produced this century about the Yukon, but most have left the territory frozen in time. "North to the Klondike" is just one of a string of films that barely got the Yukon beyond the gold rush. (Courtesy of the Anchorage Museum)*

ABOVE: *It seems the Yukon was a bit too far for most Hollywood studios, but Universal-International did claim to film "The Far Country" in the "Great Canadian Northwest." (Courtesy of the Anchorage Museum)*

TOP RIGHT: *James Oliver Curwood's novels sprang off the big screen in abundance. Panned by many critics, Curwood's novels nonetheless solidified the image of the Yukon in the mind of most viewers. (Courtesy of the Anchorage Museum)*

North by reading Jack London stories and Robert Service poems. Therefore, movies released during the next 10 years included "The Call of the Wild" (1923), "The Law of the Yukon" (1920), and two versions of "The Shooting of Dan McGrew" (1915, 1924).

Most northern movies, unfortunately, were based on literature that was something less than distinguished. James Oliver Curwood was the major purveyor of northern movie material during the 1920s, and on the basis of sheer volume alone he cannot be ignored: He wrote 26 novels and contributed to more than 100 motion pictures. No wonder a reviewer dubbed him "the prize literary hustler on the continent." Audiences enjoyed and critics hated his movies, which were usually a tepid melange of stout-hearted Mounties and happy-go-lucky fur trappers. Film historian Jim Hitt concluded that "Curwood did not write any great or near-great novels, and the films based on his work reflect his lack of talent."

During the 1920s, Hollywood produced more than 50 silent movies with a gold rush theme. Of those, two were surprisingly good. "The Trail of '98," a 1929 film based on

Robert Service's only northern novel, was a romantic melodrama praised for its authenticity; Pierre Berton has noted that it was one of the few northern pictures in which the stampeders looked the part. And in 1925, "The Gold Rush" was released. Charlie Chaplin was the director and star in what has been hailed as one of the artistic triumphs of the silent film era; Chaplin himself considered it the film for which he wanted to be remembered. Most of the scenery is stereotypical, with plasterboard mountains, tame bears and an eternally snowbound landscape. But the geography didn't matter; what was important was its statement on the human condition, all based on the familiar Klondike backdrop.

With the onset of the Great Depression, silent movies gave way to "talkies," and studios were forced to cut costs. The decade of the 1930s, therefore, was the golden age of the low-budget, "B" movie western, and many less-than-memorable movies were made about the North. Rex Beach's book *The Barrier* (1908), released as a "Klondike" movie in 1937, was criticized as "truly laughable," with errors "too numerous to mention." Five years later came "North to the Klondike," which featured "an unbelievable rehash of the same old stereotyped characters." And in 1943 "Klondike Kate" was released, complete with a Yukon lynching scene. The Royal Canadian

BELOW LEFT : *Not surprisingly, Dawson figured prominently in many films about the Yukon. Diamond Tooth Gertie's, an entertainment establishment in present-day Dawson, carries on the tradition brought to the big screen in RKO Radio Pictures's "Belle of the Yukon." (Courtesy of the Anchorage Museum)*

BELOW: *In selecting a title for their film, the producers of "The Law of the North" managed to avoid the three most common words assigned to films about the Yukon: Arctic, Klondike, Yukon. (Courtesy of the Anchorage Museum)*

Mounted Police, one of Hollywood's favorite subjects, got so annoyed at the way movies treated them that it sent a former officer, Bruce Carruthers, to Hollywood as a technical advisor. Carruthers tried to correct the worst of the errors, but often he was told, "Ah, nobody'll ever know the difference."

Cost prohibited most producers from filming on location in the Yukon. When Austen "Cap" Lathrop, prominent Alaska businessman and filmmaker, decided to produce his version of "The Cheechakos," he filmed the Chilkoot Pass scenes at Bartlett Glacier south of Portage in southcentral Alaska. (B84-118-68, The Anchorage Museum)

The writing and acting could be bad, but Hollywood's sense of geography could be even worse. "Call of the Yukon," a 1938 production based on a Curwood novel, was actually set on the arctic coast of Alaska and filmed somewhere in California. A 1939 film "North of the Yukon" featured a French-Canadian trapper. The 1936 Mae West hit, "Klondike Annie," was set in and around Nome, Alaska.

When it came to movies, the title meant everything, and certain key words were used repeatedly to convey both a sense of place and a sense of excitement. Shows about Canada typically referred to "God's Country" or "Land of the Big Snows," and in reference to movies about the Yukon, the most common words were "Arctic," "Klondike" and "Yukon." Half or more of north country feature films released between 1930 and 1955 had one of these three words in the title.

A takeoff on the northern movie was the serial. These productions had been part of moviemaking since the silent film era, and serials about the Mounties had been around since the early 1930s. The studios liked serials because, like "B" movies, they were produced quickly and cheaply. In 1945, Universal released "The Royal Mounted Rides Again," which featured several episodes in a mythical region called "Canaska," perched somewhere along the 141st meridian. Three years later another serial, "Dangers of the Royal Mounted," was set in the town of "Alcana." Two other serials followed; the most popular was "Sergeant Preston of the Yukon," which played from 1955 to 1958.

Production companies knew that the most vivid way to exhibit the north country was to shoot films on location. Few, however, brought a crew to the Yukon; the time and expenses involved prevented it. Moviemakers, therefore, had to simulate the area's scenery. One of the most recognizable north country scenes, for example, was the panoramic view of stampeders climbing Chilkoot Pass in the spring of 1898. The pass, however, was relatively inaccessible, so Charlie Chaplin shot the opening scenes of "The Gold Rush" near Lake Tahoe and Austen "Cap" Lathrop, pioneer Alaska businessman and filmmaker, chose Bartlett Glacier, south of Portage, for "The Cheechakos."

During the years following World War II, the face of Hollywood began to change. The "B" movie began to decline because of increased costs, and by the early 1950s television was a viable competitor to the local movie house. The predominant theme of northern movies, however, continued to be gold rush-era westerns. Of the 70 northern feature films produced between 1910 and 1955, some 50 of them were set in the gold rush. To a large extent, they were the same dreary affairs cranked out during the 1930s and early 1940s. Monogram Pictures, a producer of second features, was apparently so pressed for cash that it released six almost identical gold-rush movies between 1949 and 1954. Monogram gave its potboilers dramatic if interchangeable titles such as "Call of the Klondike," "Fangs of the Arctic," "Trail of the Yukon" or "Yukon Vengeance," but the movies really had nothing to do with the Klondike, the Yukon or the Arctic. Kirby Grant, on contract to Monogram at the time, starred in all of them.

Such behavior might be expected from a "B" studio, but Universal-International was just as reckless in its presentation of "The Far Country" (1954), which starred James Stewart and Walter Brennan. Dismissed by the critics as "juvenile claptrap," Pierre Berton lambasted it for its historical inaccuracies — everything from a gunfight on the streets of Dawson City to Chilkats inhabiting the upper Pelly River. It also featured a Dawson scene in which a Mountie asked a group of prospectors to elect themselves a U.S. Marshal.

The director of "The Far Country" chose Athabasca Glacier in Alberta as the site for some scenes for his film. (Courtesy of the Anchorage Museum)

Since 1955, few movies have been produced with a Yukon setting. Some, such as "The Savage Innocents" (1959), "Mara of the Wilderness" (1965), or "Never Cry Wolf" (1982) tried to be consciousness-raising. "Klondike Fever" (1981) and "White Fang" (1991) have been traditional gold rush stories. "Northern Exposure," the recent television series, showed the quirky side of northern life; though light-hearted, it pointed out some real, if hidden, attributes of northern communities.

It would be tempting to conclude that because recent movies have been more realistic than those shown before 1955, Hollywood has therefore seen the error of its ways and will henceforth aim toward true interpretations of the Yukon's people and environment. Such a conclusion, however, is both unrealistic and a trifle misguided. Historians and other moviegoers need to recognize that most, if not all, northern movies will continue to emphasize unique aspects of northern life. We can only hope that the current trend toward cinematic honesty continues. ●

Today

By Yvette Brend

Over the years, Emile Lévèsque's hair has faded in color from flaming red to snowy white, his nerves have buckled from too many 18-hour days of hard toil, and his hearing is failing. But the miner's eyes still sparkle like tiny flecks of Yukon gold, and his freckled face takes on a strange fire when talk turns to the veins of ore that beckoned this maritimer to the Canadian North, like thousands of stampeders before him. "It's the gold....It does something to people," he said, pouring a pile of misshapen, straw-colored nuggets into his palm.

An estimated 30,000 people filled the streets of Dawson City a century ago, building roads and towns along their way. Some of those settlements are now just memories. Others, like the Yukon Territory capital of Whitehorse, survived and grew. Gold, copper and other minerals still fuel the territory's economy, but more and more people work for the government or tourism industry. Agriculture is even enjoying unprecedented growth, with the number of farms tripling and with crops ranging from feed hay and highland cattle to elk. Velvet-covered antlers are clipped from the elk, then processed into ingredients for pills and exotic potions.

For Emile Lévèsque the land remains rich with the promise of fortune. He is one of a dwindling group of placer miners who live the old way, chewing up the ground, guiding the rocks through a shaker, a wash plant and ultimately swirling out the heavy gold in a hand-held pan.

Lévèsque waits for the old-timers and absent "southerners" to give up their land. He is slowly buying up claims in the heart of gold rush country, near a frontier mining center turned tourism hot-spot, Dawson City.

Yukon Territory becomes less remote every year with cheaper charter flights from Vancouver and Europe, computer links, satellite dishes, ski-doo®s, four-wheelers and even rumors of a road branching off the Dempster Highway to Old Crow.

According to Lévèsque, the rolling, spruce-choked hills of the northern Yukon are still rich with everything from wildlife to archaeological treasures. The land he prods and blasts with high-pressured bursts of water has seen many shifts and changes throughout the centuries. Some 70,000 years ago, when half-mile-thick ice blanketed most of North America, one corner of the continent remained ice free. This section of land, including part of Alaska and the upper half of the Yukon, joined the Siberian tundra via a land bridge and was known as Beringia. Beringia offered a home to oversized creatures: bear-sized beavers, sabre-toothed cats and woolly mammoths among them. The ancestors of today's aboriginal Yukoners hunted these massive mammals.

FACING PAGE: *The Yukon Government Building, Rotary Peace Park and the S.S.* Klondike *highlight this view of downtown Whitehorse.* (Alissa Crandall)

Dancing girls celebrate Canada Day, July 1, with a Mountie in Dawson. (George Matz)

Combing the earth around the old capital of the Klondike, Lévèsque has found much evidence of the past near Hester Creek, from 8-foot-long (2.4 m.) ivory mammoth tusks to giant beaver dams preserved in the permafrost 70 feet (21 m.) underground. The New Brunswick-born miner has sold most of his ivory finds to jewelers and carvers. He has kept some of his freeze-dried trophies, lacquering the mammoth jaws and molars with resin. Lévèsque doesn't tell too many people about his finds. He doesn't want any high-minded scientists shutting down his digs. "I'm there for the gold," says the 54-year-old with no plans for retirement.

Lévèsque says that today's technology allows him to find riches in the piles left behind by the miners. "I've done real well cleaning up other people's rock piles, but it's hard to get ground. People hold onto it." All he needs is more time, he says.

Lévèsque is a living reminder of the Yukon of old, but the Canadian territory is no longer just a land of prospectors, log cabins and caribou hunting.

In the capital city of Whitehorse, where almost three-quarters of the population lives, there are Internet providers and four fast-food restaurants, including McDonald's and KFC. Even in Dawson, population 2,151, about 165 miles (264 km.) south of the Arctic Circle, there is a bank machine and modern hotels.

Lévèsque has a house in Dawson where his wife, Collette, has a huge sewing room and a myriad of gold baubles. She manages her husband's books and runs the orderly household. In November 1997, Lévèsque sat watching his big-screen television, while his teen-age son Andie played Nintendo with a friend after they finished some riffs on an electric guitar. Andie has no interest in taking over his father's life work. "I guess I've just seen too much of mining," said the teen, turning for a moment from his joystick, a tuque hugging his ear-ringed ears. When bored, the boys head out to snowmobile among the hills flanking Dawson, one of 32 settlements peppered across Yukon Territory. These pockets of people, from the eight official residents of Champagne Landing to the 24,031 people living in Whitehorse, are spread across a land mass large enough to encompass the U.S. states of California, Arizona, Delaware and West Virginia. The roughly triangular shape of Yukon Territory spans 193,380 square miles (483,450 sq. km.), stretching from the 60th parallel (about the latitude of Ninilchik on Alaska's Kenai Peninsula and Stockholm, Sweden) to the Beaufort Sea.

Yukon Native history dates back to the last ice age and offers a rich tapestry of some 14 First Nations that speak more than seven different languages. Until the 1950s there was a permanent population on the north slope, but now the territory's northern coastal tundra is devoid of settlements. Its interior forests have been peopled for thousands of years by Athabaskans, which today fall into six distinct groups including the Kutchin, Han, Tutchone, Inland Tlingit, Kaska and Tagish. About a quarter of the Yukon population are First Nation people, most living in outlying communities. According to 1997 Yukon Bureau of Statistics figures, the communities with the highest aboriginal populations include Burwash Landing (population 88), Carcross (population 431), Carmacks (population 478), Mayo (population 507), Old Crow (population 305), Pelly Crossing (population 299) and Ross River (population 437).

Most smaller Yukon settlements have little cash economy, but residents trap or hunt everything from muskrat on the flats of Old

BELOW LEFT: *Betty and Ed Karman of Haines Junction relax by an old car that Ed hopes to fix up. One of the original construction workers on the Alaska Highway, Ed and his wife were elected Mr. and Mrs. Yukon by the Yukon Order of Pioneers several years ago. (Alissa Crandall)*

BELOW: *These youngsters have their own ice cream social at Carcross. Formerly known as Caribou Crossing, the town sits astride a caribou migration route between Lake Bennett and Nares Lake. (Harry M. Walker)*

FACING PAGE: *The Whitehorse Orchestra performs at the Yukon Arts Centre with Whitehorse in the background.* (Cathie Archbould)

RIGHT: *This log building is the downtown Whitehorse terminal for the White Pass & Yukon Route railroad that runs from Skagway on Alaska's Inside Passage to the Yukon capital. The line was completed July 29, 1900, and was designed to help miners and suppliers reach the Yukon Valley without the steep hike over the mountains or the slow boat ride up the Yukon River.* (Cathie Archbould)

Crow to moose, Dall sheep, snowshoe hare or even the odd grouse around Whitehorse. In summer, most everyone is armed with rod and reel to hook the grayling, arctic char and rainbow trout stocked in the lakes and rivers. Yukon waterways are naturally populated with northern pike or "jack fish," trout, whitefish and grayling. The rainbow trout and arctic char populations are boosted by government restocking programs in designated lakes. By summer's end, hooked-nose salmon – heavier than overweight house cats – fight their way up the Yukon River and its tributaries to expand a fisherman's options.

The economies of the larger communities of Whitehorse, Carmacks and Faro are fueled by mines, which in late 1997 were facing an uncertain future with the worldwide dip in gold and copper prices.

Some Yukon residents are turning to the land in a different way, selling the mystique of the North to tourists yearning to kayak, hike or mush their way through the wilds.

Dog mushers spend their entire year preparing for the annual 1,000-mile (1,600-km.) Yukon Quest sled dog race that follows the old gold rush routes of the 1800s. Commonly referred to simply as the Quest, the race alternates direction, beginning one year in Whitehorse and ending in Fairbanks, Alaska, and reversing direction the following year. For many Yukoners, from the mushers to the trappers and miners, the traditional dream of an arctic life lives on, with the help of modern conveniences such as fleece and Sorel® boots.

For Emile Lévèsque and his employee, Barney Lauzon, 49, it is clear the newcomers are changing the way of the Yukon. In Lévèsque's view, there are more rules now in Dawson. No open liquor in the streets. A hardware store. People walk the streets sipping lattes from the Riverwest Food and Health store, where teachers and government workers leave their shiny new Nissan Pathfinders and Ford Explorers idling outside. Lauzon remembers when the Yukon River ran the color of mud from placer mining effluent. *National Geographic*® photographed a drunk leaning in a hotel alley, a bottle of Bourbon in one hand and a bottle of

Lemon Gin in the other. Few boozers and druggies lurch along the streets these days. "The tourists don't like to see that," said Lauzon. "We're in a transition period. It's more tourist-oriented here now."

Lévèsque and Lauzon have seen the focus of Dawson change. They've seen the cheechakos (newcomers) come and go while sourdoughs hang tough through 40 below temperatures and the floods that moved houses in 1979. But now the newcomers are fixing up the buildings and entertaining more Germans and other Europeans in polished, $100-per-night hotel rooms. The town still has a few rough edges. There are those who steal gold from Lévèsque's sluice box or salt claims to sell their mines for inflated prices.

Yukon Territory was partially shaped by those who came seeking gold. Although Whitehorse is now the hub of the roads crisscrossing the territory, the city began as a stopover on the route to Klondike gold. Upon completion of the White Pass & Yukon Route railway, connecting Skagway, Alaska, with the Yukon River, Whitehorse became a transport terminus for river steamers and stampeders. Thousands landed in Whitehorse to dry out after running nearby rapids. The foamy white water looked like the manes of so many white horses, so the city got its name. The rapids disappeared after Northern Canada Power Commission built a hydroelectric dam on the river. Now Whitehorse is the home of the legislative buildings, most territorial and federal government offices and the law courts. The city offers gourmet restaurants, two movie theaters and a main street that bustles with Birkenstock-shod backpackers and Tommy Hilfiger-clad tourists in July. Buses still stop over in the dusty city on tours around Yukon Territory, which receives less annual rainfall than Arizona.

Just 44 miles (70 km.) south of Whitehorse, another stop along the route to the gold fields intersected with a common caribou migration path. Carcross, formerly called Caribou Crossing, was a major stop on the rail route from 1900 to 1982. Rumors are that after a 16-year lull, the train from Skagway may again run to Carcross in the summer of

LEFT: *Karen Bricken enjoys the cross-country skiing trails of Miles Canyon. (Matt McGovern-Rowen)*

FACING PAGE: *Joyce Majiski climbs a rock face above Lowell Glacier in the Alsek Valley. (Cathie Archbould)*

ABOVE LEFT: *Baking day stirs Ellen Davignon in her kitchen at Johnson's Crossing. (Alissa Crandall)*

ABOVE: *Danny Roberts views the Yukon from his home at Fort Selkirk. (Laurent Dick)*

1998. The White Pass and Yukon Route Corp. ran the train to Whitehorse in July 1997 as part of the Ton of Gold celebration, attracting cheering train buffs and history lovers. Descendants of the original stampeders gathered there to re-enact the delivery of the first shipment of gold.

Around the turn of the century, goldseekers took the same path the railroad subsequently followed in their efforts to reach the Klondike, except they walked. Even after the line was built, many would-be gold kings loaded supplies on their back and hiked the 33-mile (53-km.) Chilkoot Trail, running from Dyea near the head of Southeast Alaska's Inside Passage over 3,739-foot-high (1,994 m.)Chilkoot Pass to Lake Bennett. Now all that is left of their toil are their rusted tools, memoirs, photographs and the history of their trek.

The territory is filled with reminders that the Yukon was built of gold. In Dawson City, the tools of the modern gold trade are exchanged, bartered and sold. On a bar wall there are notices of equipment for sale. This day it's a 1994 Arctic Cat® snowmachine with hand/thumb warmers, 1,100 "soft" miles (1,760 km.), for $3,200.

Across the Yukon, place names hearken back to the romance and simplicity of the time when Dawson was borne out of a mosquito-infested bog. There is Champagne

Deb Gutra and Dave Gilbert serve travelers at Jake's Corner, at the junction of the Alaska Highway and the road to Atlin Lake. A spur connects Jake's Corner with the Klondike Highway running north from Skagway to Whitehorse. (Ed Steele)

Landing, where it's rumored a case of the bubbly beverage was found a century ago. The creeks – Deadman, Christmas, Goldbottom and Scurvy, to name a few – tell of the riches or tragedy found on their banks.

Lévèsque still uncovers the odd foot bone from one of the hard-working pack horses who helped haul the "silver-dollar" riveted shovels and supplies to camp. One time he reopened a mine shaft and found a frozen wool shirt, still marked with the Chinese symbols from a Dawson laundry that operated 100 years ago.

But what of dreams of riches when the price of gold dips to a little more than $3 per ounce and the mines grind to a halt? The romance of the glowing golden stones is no longer the main thrust of the territory. Young Yukoners are heading off to southern universities or looking to other industries for their future. Most know the search for gold is a tough, uncompromising slog through mud, gravel and permafrost, and often lonely. "You don't get nothing without hard work," says Lévèsque, who like many miners, claims there is still a fortune in the hills and valleys of parts of the Yukon. "If I'd only started

FACING PAGE: *Ken Madsen and a companion canoe the Takhini River, a Yukon River tributary that begins in Kusawa Lake. The river is known for a hot springs near its mouth, just upriver on the Yukon from Lake Laberge. Chinook salmon spawn in the Takhini.* (George Wuerthner)

ABOVE: *Theo Rennick fishes the Ogilvie River along the Dempster corridor in northcentral Yukon.* (Penny Rennick)

ABOVE RIGHT: *Woodchopping is a daily chore for many Yukoners.* (Robert Hahn)

younger, I'd be a billionaire now," he laughs.

Even in their heyday, the gold fields left many broke, disillusioned or dead. The youth of Dawson see little allure in the glitter that attracted so many young fortune-seekers 10 decades ago. They want jobs, university degrees and computer training. In downtown Dawson, the Robert Service School is brimming with more than 300 students. There are more and more families moving to town, and fewer miners every year. Last winter dozens of young athletes from all areas of the territory gathered for a volleyball tournament. Whitehorse-born Justin Van Fleet looked on as a yellow-jerseyed teen spiked the ball at her opponent. Van Fleet is apprenticing to be a carpenter. The 20-year-old, of Han ancestry, is one of a new wave of First Nations youth armed with education, direction and, for many, a reborn awareness of culture. "I don't get much into (my culture), but that's just me," he says. Van Fleet now lives in Dawson City, where he has helped build leeching pads for gold operations. The pads are flat surfaces

LEFT: *Nicholas Vanier arrives at Pelly Crossing during the Yukon Quest sled dog race. (Laurent Dick)*

ABOVE: *Musher Frank Turner saw his training efforts at his sled dog kennel pay off when he won the Yukon Quest. (Laurent Dick)*

BELOW: *Barney Lauzon (right) and Emile Lévèsque discuss their years of mining in the Klondike at Lévèsque's home in Dawson. (Yvette Brend)*

FACING PAGE: *Three teams travel the Yukon River downriver from Whitehorse during the 1997 Yukon Quest. The 1,000-mile (1,600 km.) race runs between Whitehorse and Fairbanks, Alaska, reversing direction each year. (Laurent Dick)*

LEFT: *During the gold rush, miners had to grow their own fresh vegetables. Decades of practice have enabled Yukoners to refine their horticultural techniques until today they produce eye-catching broccoli, zucchini, carrots and other vegetables.* (Joyce Majiski)

FACING PAGE: *Laurent Dick displays a portion of a harvest of morel mushrooms at a camp off the Top of the World Highway. Morel mushrooms sprout in burned areas in incredible numbers the first year after a forest fire. The mushrooms are processed in food dryers and some of this harvest was sold to a buyer from British Columbia. In good years, mushroom pickers can earn a few thousand dollars for their efforts.* (Courtesy of Laurent Dick)

where the ore is spread out and soaked with chemicals to separate the gold from rock. He is now working in construction. He plans to stay in Dawson, adding, "There's lots of work here and I'm used to this place now."

Yukon Territory is no longer some far-flung northern frontier offering only gold. It is a series of pockets of civilization linked by phones, roads (except Old Crow) and computers. Dawson City's pubs and hostelry crawl with placer miners who sit alongside mushers, teachers and firefighters and enjoy a beer. Tourists, who flock to Dawson by the thousands in the summer, can buy the best champagne and filet mignon.

Whitehorse is even more up-to-date, with just as many bank machines and satellite dishes as most southern cities in Canada. Many professionals – doctors, lawyers, bureaucrats – come to learn their trade or work for the Yukon Territorial Government and move on.

The city, territorial capital for the past 45 years, offers all the luxuries of a seat of government. There are five media outlets: three radio stations, two newspapers, including one of the last independent Canadian dailies, the *Whitehorse Star*. There's also a modern college, international airport, hospital, retirement home, swimming pool and several grocery stores and arenas.

More elderly Yukoners are opting to stay year-round instead of heading south for the winter. The number of young families is growing also. Student enrollment in the territory's 27 schools increased to 6,476 in 1997, forcing many teachers into portables and crowded classrooms. The growing number of young families is helping to drive a system that touches an estimated 15,000 Yukoners, through enrollment or employment.

Mining is the other big economic force, with more than 30 mining-related companies operating out of Whitehorse.

Tracie Harms offers selections from Mom's Bakery at the Fox Lake Campground on the Klondike Highway. (Karen Cornelius)

The city sports a modern visitor reception center with multi-image slide presentations about the territory and attractions that range from Sam McGee's cabin to the Yukon Transportation Museum. Replicas of giant beaver and the largest woolly mammoth skeleton ever recovered grace the halls of the new Beringia Centre, where exhibits lead visitors through the Yukon as it was before recorded time.

In February, residents and visitors break up the monotony of winter with the Sourdough Rendezvous, where a queen and Sourdough Sam are crowned. In the past, rendezvous events have included everything from period costume contests to flour packing and chain saw chucking.

The Yukon is a land of characters. And flying aficionados, like Moe Grant, who use Whitehorse as a base and treat the territory as their kingdom. The 68-year-old Grant froze both his legs off from the shin down when he crashed near Atlin, B.C. one freezing February 47 years ago. The 21-year-old spent several days waiting for rescue and quickly learned to walk on prosthetics and fly again. He has spent the rest of his days winging around the Yukon, from the Alsek River to the shores of Lake Schwatka where Grant keeps his two-seater today.

Most Whitehorse-dwellers looking for a good way to while away the long hours of the cold season enjoy tamer winter sports, from downhill and cross-country skiing and snow boarding to dog mushing.

On summer weekends, city dwellers scramble for the hills and back roads, to hike, climb, cycle, or for the rushing rapids and placid lakes to wind surf, kayak, raft, canoe or fish.

For in-town entertainment, there is live theater and music, and a concert stage at Yukon College where big name performers often play. Local movie theaters offer most of the big name pictures and the odd gem of originality in film festivals.

For the athlete, Whitehorse is a city of action. For the sedentary, the dusty summers and dark winters can drag a bit.

Other towns are growing with the promise of renewed mining. The population of Faro jumped to 1,266 in 1997 after hints that

The grand riverboats of an earlier time did not lack for elegance, as this photo of the dining room of the S.S. Klondike proves. Completion of the White Pass & Yukon Route rail line prompted the British-owned company to enter the river commerce business. Whitehorse became winter quarters for the British Yukon Navigation Co. fleet, which, either directly or through offshoots, operated steamers on navigable waters throughout the territory. (George Wuerthner)

the Anvil Range Mining Corp. would restart production. As of spring 1998 this has yet to happen, but hope remains.

Other communities dwindle or turn to social assistance with the ebb and flow of mining-related employment. About 600 people lived in Elsa, a tiny community near the Keno Hill Mine, about 45 miles north of Mayo. When the mine collapsed in 1989, most left. Two months later there were less than a dozen, said Geordie Dobson, 72, owner of the Keno City Hotel and tale-spinner extraordinaire. "Usually there are rumors, but in this case it was 'boom' that's it," said the old-timer, who lives on the cusp of the wilderness. He came in 1954 to mine after years as a merchant sailor. He's been thrice married and around the globe more times than he can count, but he would never leave the Yukon wilderness now. "I ran away to go to sea at 15. I've worked in every country

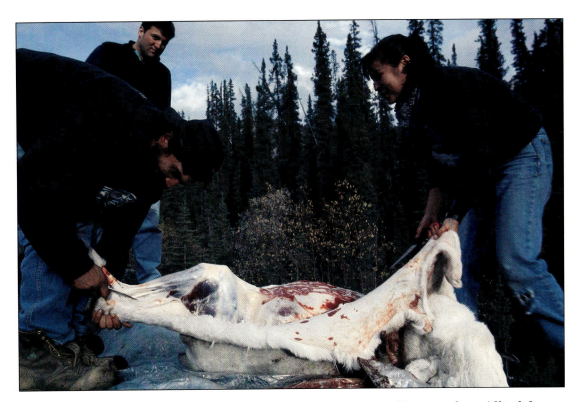

FACING PAGE: *Long a landmark at Watson Lake, this signpost acknowledges decades of Alaska Highway travels. (Alissa Crandall)*

ABOVE: *Will Carey watches Gwitch'in Patsy Chudy and Terry Close of Dawson skin a Dall sheep. (Edward Steele)*

ABOVE RIGHT: *Andie Lévèsque poses with a mammoth bone retrieved from one of his father's mining efforts. (Yvette Brend)*

under the sun," says the hotelier, who might give a traveler a deal on a room if he takes a shine to him. Dobson says he recalls floating off the coast of Japan when Allied forces dropped the bomb on Hiroshima, 500 miles (800 km.) away. He recounts with relish a night in a South African cell, next to a cannibal who claimed he ate his aunt. He remembers when there were no tourists, just miners, in the Yukon. Now Elsa can't sustain a pizza parlor and most of the handful of residents survive on welfare. "I've worked all over on rigged ships...but when I came here I thought, Jesus, this is the place," referring to the pristine lakes ripe with fish. "I want for nothing and I can still satisfy a woman...when I capture one," he joked.

When the communities do die out, the people go back to their bush camps or go south to Whitehorse, or to Alberta or British Columbia. They travel with resumés almost as varied as that of Jack London. The unofficial chronicler of the Klondike, who captured the feel of the land in his words, also worked as everything from a prospector to a war correspondent. Today, second-generation miner Dean Klassen feels like he is in the same boat. He and his siblings took over their parent's Dawson-area mine years ago. After summers of driving heavy equipment, they are sick of trying to extract life from the land and living at the whim of world

ALASKA GEOGRAPHIC® 123

gold prices. So the Clear Water Creek cat-mining property is for sale to anybody with $1.5 million. When it goes, Klassen will move on. "My resumé reads like a phone book," says the man who has done everything from build roads to weld his own heavy machinery. Does he plan to leave the Yukon? No. Unthinkable to a real Yukoner. "It's a big piece of ground," he jokes. "I'll find something." ●

The Robert Service School in Dawson commemorates one of the Yukon's literary legends. Service lived in Dawson from 1909 to 1912, during which time he wrote a novel and continued to produce his poetry. (Yukon Government)

Bibliography

Cinq-Mars, Jacques. "Bluefish Cave 1: A Late Pleistocene Eastern Beringian Cave Deposit in the Northern Yukon." *Canadian Journal of Archaeology* 3:1-32. 1979.

Clark, Donald W. *Western Arctic Prehistory*. Hull: Canadian Museum of Civilization. 1991.

–. "Fort Reliance, Yukon: An Archaeological Assessment." *Canadian Museum of Civilization Mercury Series, Archaeological Survey of Canada* Paper No. 150. 1995.

Coutts, R.C. *Yukon Places and Names*. Sidney, British Columbia: Gray's Publishing Ltd., 1980.

Dobrowolsky, Helene. *Law of the Yukon*. Whitehorse: Lost Moose Yukon Publishers, 1995.

Doogan, Mike. *Dawson City*. Anchorage: Alaska Geographic Society, 1988.

Gotthardt, Ruth. "The Archaeological Sequence in the Northern Cordillera: A Consideration of Typology and Traditions." *Occasional Papers in Archaeology* No. 1. Whitehorse: Yukon Heritage Branch, 1990.

Greer, Sheila. *Skookum Stories on the Chilkoot/Dyea Trail*. Whitehorse: Carcross-Tagish First Nation, 1995.

– and Raymond J. LeBlanc. "Yukon Culture History: an Update." *The Musk-Ox* Vol. 33:26-36, 1983.

Hare, P. Gregory. "Holocene Occupations in the Southern Yukon: New Perspectives from the Annie Lake Site." *Occasional Papers in Archaeology* No. 5. Whitehorse: Yukon Heritage Branch, 1995.

Hartmier, Richard. *Yukon, Color of the Land*. Whitehorse: Lost Moose, The Yukon Publishers, 1995.

Irving, William N. and Jacques Cinq-Mars. "A Tentative Archaeological Sequence for Old Crow Flats, Yukon Territory." *Arctic Anthropology* Vol. 11 (supplement): 65-81. 1974.

LeBlanc, Raymond J. "The Rat Indian Creek Site and the Late Prehistoric Period in the Interior Northern Yukon." *National Museum of Man Mercury Series, Archaeological Survey of Canada* Paper No. 120. 1984.

MacNeish, Richard E. "Men out of Asia: as seen from the Northwest Yukon." *Anthropological Papers of the University of Alaska* 7(2):41-70. 1959.

–. "Investigations in Southwest Yukon: Archaeological Excavation, Comparisons and Speculations." *Papers of the Robert S. Peabody Foundation for Archaeology*, Vol. 6 No. 2, pp. xiii + 199-488. Andover: Phillips Academy, 1964.

McGhee, Robert. *Canadian Arctic Prehistory*. Hull: Canadian Museum of Civilization, 1990.

Morlan, Richard E. "The Later Prehistory of the Middle Porcupine Drainage, Northern Yukon Territory." *National Museum of Man Mercury Series, Archaeological Survey of Canada* Paper No. 11. 1978.

– and Jacques Cinq-Mars. "Ancient Beringians: Human Occupations in the Late Pleistocene of Alaska and the Yukon Territory." In *Paleoecology of Beringia*, D.B. Hopkins, J.V. Matthews, Jr., C.E. Schweger and S.B. Young, editors, pp. 353-382. New York: Academic Press, 1982.

– and William B. Workman. "Prehistoric Man in the Southwest Yukon." In *Kluane Pinnacle of the Yukon*, John Theberge, editor, pp. 97-107. Toronto and Garden City: Doubleday, 1980.

Neufeld, David. "Trampled In The Rush." in *Legion Magazine*, January/February 1998.

Page, John W. and Jill De La Hunt. *Exploring The Alaska-Yukon Bordercountry*. Minocqua, WI: NorthWord Press, Inc., 1994.

Ray, Delia. *Gold! The Klondike Adventure*. New York: Lodestar Books, E.P. Dutton, 1989.

Rennick, Penny, editor. *Prehistoric Alaska*. Anchorage: Alaska Geographic Society, 1994.

Workman, William B. "Prehistory of the Aishihik-Kluane Area, Southwest Yukon Territory." *National Museum of Man Mercury Series, Archaeological Survey of Canada* Paper No. 74. 1978.

Index

30-Mile Section (of Yukon River) 16, 46
Abel, Charlie 67
Abel, Sarah 60-67
Aberdeen Canyon 16
Abbott, Grant 75
Agriculture 24, 25, 104, 118
Alaska (Alcan) Highway 4, 19, 35, 113, 122
Ancestral Dené 52, 54, 55, 56
Animals 2, 12, 14, 25-27, 32, 33, 39, 40, 43, 45, 46, 50, 55, 56, 60, 63, 67, 107, 109, 123
Anvil Range Mining Corp. 77, 79, 121
Arctic National Wildlife Refuge 43
Arctic Small Tool tradition 56
Athabaskans 107
Atkinson, Mary (Laferte) 89, 91, 92, 95
Atkinson, William (Billy) 89, 91, 92, 97
Atna Resources 79
Attaway, Michael 70

Back, Frank 92
Back, Capt. Henry S. 92
Beach, Rex 101
Beads, Elizabeth 86
Beads, John 86
Beaver Creek (town) 6
Bee, Austin 92
Bee, Tom 92, 93, 94
Beringia 19, 22-24, 43, 45, 50, 104
Beringia Centre 2, 23, 120
Berton, Pierre 101, 103
Bierlmeier, Linda 2
Birds 16, 17, 19, 20, 21, 25-27, 37, 40, 43, 45-47
Blackstone Uplands 22, 46
Blind Creek 83
Bluefish Caves 22, 50
Bob, Liard 88
Bouvette, Louis 76

Brend, Yvette 2, 60
Brennan, Walter 103
Brenner, Diane 2
Bricken, Karen 110
British Mountains 8, 22, 40, 43
British Yukon Navigation Co. 121
Brown, Afe 93
Bruce, Robert 67
Burins 56, 59
Burwash Landing 107
Buttle, Roy 89
BYG Natural Resources Ltd. 68

Campbell, Robert 82, 84-88
Canyon City 50
Carcross 24, 25, 107, 110
Carey, Will 122
Carmack, George 68, 70-73
Carmacks (community) 55, 56, 68, 91-94, 107, 109
Carruthers, Bruce 102
Champagne Landing 106, 112
Chaplin, Charlie 101
Charlie, Alfred 62
Chick, Molly 4
Chilkoot Pass 71, 84, 102, 112
Chilkoot Trail 47, 112
Christie, J.M. 80
Chudy, Patsy 123
Clark, Dr. Donald W. 2
Close, Terry 123
Coal River Springs 40, 45
Coal River Springs Ecological Reserve 47
Cominco Ltd. 76, 77, 79
Copper working 54-56
Cornelius, Don 45
Cornelius, Mandy 45
Corning, Red 80
Coté, Joe 82, 88, 92, 93, 97
Curwood, James Oliver 100

Dalton, Jack 35
Daughtry, Capt. A. F. 84

Davignon, Ellen 112
Dawson City 4, 11, 24, 46, 70, 71, 73, 80, 82, 88, 92, 94, 101, 103, 104, 106, 110, 112, 113, 115, 116, 118
Dawson Creek, British Columbia 4
Dawson Daily News 80, 83
Dawson, George Mercer 71
Denali culture 53
Dempster Highway 19, 22, 23, 46, 104
Diamond Tooth Gertie's 101
Dick, Laurent 118
Dobson, Geordie 121, 122
Drury, John 84
Drury, William 84, 89, 91, 94
Duke of Abruzzi 37

Elsa 79, 121, 122
Enevoldsen (Envoldsen), Fred 82, 83, 88, 91, 92, 94, 95
Enevoldsen, Mary 88, 91
Etzel, Frank 93

Faro 77, 79, 109, 121
Fast Facts 17
Field, Edward 87
Field, Kittie (Tom) 88-92
Field, Poole 84, 87-92, 94, 97
Field, Sir Frederick Laurie 87
Field, Tannie 89, 92
Films 98-103
First Nations 4, 42, 50, 67, 107, 115
Firth, John 40
Fish 16, 26, 33, 47, 64, 109, 115
Fishing Branch River Ecological Reserve 43
Five Finger Rapids 11
Flint Creek phase 50
Forests 23, 24, 29, 32
Fort Halkett 87
Fort McPherson 87
Fort Norman 88, 93
Fort Selkirk 86, 87, 112
Fort Simpson 86, 87, 93, 94
Fort Yukon 87
Frost, Dennis 63
Fungi, bird's nest 29

Geology 19, 39, 45, 75
Gilbert, Dave 113
Glaciers 10, 16, 19, 36, 39, 50, 75

Grant, Kirby 103
Grant, Moe 120
Guder, Paul Fritz 92-94
Gutra, Deb 113
Gwitch'in Ancient Voices Camp 54

Haines Highway 35
Haines Junction 6, 24, 30, 35, 107
Harkin, Bud 83
Harms, Tracie 120
Hart, Craig 2
Hawksley, John 93
Hay River 94
Henderson, Robert (Bob) 70, 82, 83
Herschel Island 6, 27, 43-45, 49
Hitt, Jim 100
Hollywood 98, 102, 103
Hoole Canyon 82-84, 88, 91, 92
Hootalinqua 80, 85
Horrigan, Capt. Fitz 88
Hudson's Bay Co. 40, 59, 60, 65, 82, 85-88

Ijutth, 88
Inuit 59
Inuvialuit First Nation 42
Ivvavik National Park 40, 42, 45
Ivvavik, meaning of 40

Jacobs, Mina 2
Jake's Corner 113
Janssen, Louie 36
Johnson's Crossing 19, 112
Jonathan, Blind Creek 88
Josie, Dolly 65
Josie, Edith 6
Josie, Erica 67
Josie, Lena 62, 65

Kagan, Dr. Norman E. 2, 80
Karman, Betty 107
Karman, Ed 107
Kempstead, Jim 2
Keno (community) 76
Keno Hill 77, 121
Ketza Creek 80, 83
Ketza River mine 68
Kipling, Rudyard 87
Klassen, Dean 123

Klondike gold rush 6, 10, 11, 35, 68, 70, 71, 73, 75, 98, 103
Klondike Highway 39, 46, 76, 77, 94, 113, 120
Kluane Game Sanctuary 35
Kluane National Park 24, 26, 30-39, 40, 46, 47
Kluane, meaning of 34
Krahn, Ed 2
Kwatlati, Elisha 64

Lachapelle, Dr. James Omar 91, 93, 94
Ladue, Joe 93
Laferte, Mary 89
Lakes
  Atlin 17, 113
  Bennett 17, 107, 112
  Dezadeash 24, 26, 35
  Emerald 39
  Fox 8
  Frances 87
  Grizzly 19
  Kathleen 33, 35
  Kluane 6, 17, 34, 39, 56
  Kusawa 17, 115
  Laberge 17, 115
  Lowell 39
  Marsh 17
  McEvoy 88
  Nares 107
  Schwatka 120
  Sheldon 87
  Tagish 17
  Tatlmain 56
  Teslin 17, 47, 83, 84
Langham, Billy 92, 93, 94
LaRose (Rose), Oliver 83, 94
Lathrop, Austen "Cap" 102
Lauzon, Barney 110, 116
Lévèsque, Andie 106, 123
Lévèsque, Collette 106
Lévèsque, Emile 104, 106, 109, 110, 113, 116
Lewis, Angela (Ward) 89, 92
Lewis, Iris (Nugget) 90, 92
Lewis, Clement S. 83, 84, 87-91, 94
Lewis, John Travers 83
Liard Hot Springs 94
Liard Plain 17
Literature, popular 98
Little Doctor 88, 94
Locke, Sarah 2, 6

Logan Mountains 97
London, Jack 6, 98, 100, 123
Lord, Annie 63, 65

Mackenzie Mountains 8, 87, 93
Madsen, Ken 115
Majiski, Joyce 2, 110
Map 9
Martin, Eliza 65
Mayo 76, 94
McCutcheon, Steve 64, 65
McDonald, Jim 82
McDougal Family 4
McIntyre, Jim 2
McIver, Allan 86, 87
McIver, Catherine 87
McLaughlin, Jim 79
Microblades 52, 54
Miles Canyon 11
Mining Industry 68-79, 104, 118, 121
Moses, Myra 65
Moses, Peter 65
Mountains 2, 8
Mount Logan 8, 17, 26, 30, 33, 36, 37
Mount Freegold 94
Mount Nansen gold mine 68
Mount St. Elias 26, 36, 37
Mushrooms 24, 118

Nahanni House 88, 89
Nahanni Indians 87
Nansen Creek 92
National Geographic 109
Nenana culture 50
Neufeld, Dave 2, 4
Nahanni Range Road 97
Nisutlin River Delta National Wildlife Area 47
Norris, Dr. Frank 2, 98
North Canol Road 19, 97
North Ogilvie Mountains 45
Northern Archaic tradition 53, 59
Northern Canada Power Commission 110
Northern Cordilleran tradition 50, 52, 53
Northwest Microblade tradition 53
Northwest Territories 6, 42, 43, 46, 53, 59, 60, 89, 93, 95, 97

Nukon, Kenneth 65
Nukon, Marion D. 65

Ogilvie Mountains 8, 19
Ogilvie, William 71
Old Crow (community) 43, 50, 56, 60, 62-65, 104, 107, 118
Old Crow Flats 19, 22, 40, 42, 49, 59

Paleo-Arctic tradition 53
Paleo-Eskimos 56
Paleo-Indians 52
Paliser, John 87
Parks Canada 2
Peepre, Juri 2
Pelly, Sir John Henry 82
Pelly Banks 87, 88, 94
Pelly Crossing 55, 80, 94, 107, 116
Pelly Mountains 82
Percy, Walker 98
Permafrost 23, 106
Plate tectonics 75
Pleistocene Epoch 16, 23, 40, 50, 75
Precontact history 50-59

Rae, Dr. John 87
Rae, Frank 93
Railroads 73
Rampart House 40, 60
Rapids of the Drowned 87, 94
Rennick, Theo 115
Richardson Mountains 8, 43
Riel, Louis 89
Ritter, John 2
Riverboats 4, 11, 71, 80, 82-84, 92-94, 121
Rivers 10
  Alsek 32, 39, 46, 47, 110, 120
  Babbage 40
  Bonnet Plume 16, 46
  Coal 17, 47
  Dease 87
  Dezadeash 35
  Firth 24, 40, 42-44, 46, 50, 56, 95
  Fortymile 68
  Frances 17, 87, 97
  Hyland 17
  Liard 17, 80, 86, 87, 90, 93
  Mackenzie 16, 17, 43, 47, 59, 80, 86-88, 93

Macmillan 93
Malcolm 40
Nahanni 88
Ogilvie 115
Old Crow 22, 65
Peel 16, 46
Pelly 11, 80-97, 103
Porcupine 11, 23, 40, 43, 65, 87
Ross 79, 80-97
Smith 87
Snake 16
Stewart 11, 68, 94
Takhini 115
Tatshenshini 32, 46, 47
Teslin 10, 80, 84, 85
White 11, 55
Wind 16
Roberts, Danny 112
Rocky Mountain Cordillera 8
Ross River (community) 19, 68, 80-97, 107
Royal Canadian (North West) Mounted Police 44, 49, 84, 85, 88, 92, 101, 102, 106
Rutledge, J.J. 80

Sailer, Art 73, 74, 76
Sailer, Noreen 73
Sand dunes 24
Sapper Hill 22
Selkirk First Nation 56
Selwyn Mountains 8, 93, 97
Service, Robert 6, 100, 101, 124
Shakwak Trench 10
Shaw and Rowlinson, 92
Sheldon Mountain 87
Skin tanning 54
Skookum Jim, 68, 70, 71
Smith, Ben 46
Smith, Jane 94
Smith, Tom 80, 83, 84, 89, 93, 94
Smith's Landing 80, 82
Sourdough Rendezvous 120
Southern Tutchone First Nation 34
South Canol Road 19, 82
Stanier, Jack 80, 93
Steamboat, Eliza 64
Steinbachs, John 2, 68
Stewart Crossing (community) 76
Stewart, James 103

Stikine Trail 85
St. Elias Mountains 8, 26, 30, 33, 36, 47
Stringer, I.O. 90, 91
Swanson, Cecil 90-92, 95
Swanson, Enid 91

Tagish (Dawson) Charlie 68, 70
Tatshenshini-Alsek Wilderness Provincial Park 33, 34
Taylor and Drury 84, 88-92, 94, 97
Taylor, Isaac 84
Television 98-103
Teslin (community) 84
Tetshim-Gevtik 60
Timeline, prehistoric 53
Tintina Trench 10
Tlingit Indians 4, 32, 34
Tom, Kittie 88
Tombstone Mountains 2, 8, 19, 46
Tourism 110
Tourism Yukon 2
Trade 56
Tr'on dek Hwech'in First Nation 46
Tufa formations 17, 40, 45
Turner, Frank 116

United Keno Hill Mining Corp. 77, 79

Van Bibber, Ira 80, 89, 94
Van Fleet, Justin 115
Van Gorder, Del 80, 88, 94
Vanier, Nicholas 116
Viceroy Resources Ltd. 70
Volcanism 8
Vuntut Gwitch'in First Nation 42, 49, 60, 62, 63, 64
Vuntut National Park 40, 42, 49
Vuntut, meaning of 43

Wada, Jujiro 46, 93, 95
Wallace, Lila 83
Ward, Angela 89
Waltenberg, Eng. George 84
Watson Lake (community) 45, 77, 90, 122
Waugaman, Candy 2
Wernecke Mountains 8, 16, 46

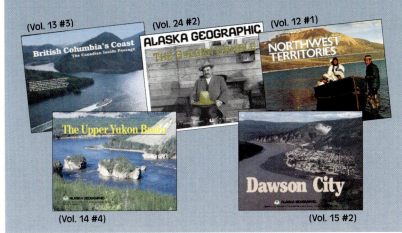

West, Mae 102
Western Cordillera 75
Westmin Mining 79
Wetlands 17, 19, 43
White Channel Gravels 75
White River volcanic ash 8, 54
White Pass & Yukon Route Railroad 4, 109, 110, 112
Whitehorse 4, 6, 11, 16, 17, 23, 25, 40, 60, 83, 94, 104, 106, 109, 110, 116, 118, 120-123
Whitehorse Star 60, 63, 68, 80, 118
Winterholt, Joe 92
World Heritage Site 34, 35

Yukon Energy Corp. 79
Yukon Geology Program 2, 75
Yukon Native Language Center 2
Yukon Order of Pioneers 107
Yukon Parks 2
Yukon Quest 109, 116
Yukon Relativity 10

Yukon River 4, 6, 10, 11, 16, 17, 26, 70, 85, 86, 109, 110, 116
Yukon Territory
  population 17, 106, 107
  size 6, 17, 107
  climate 6

PHOTOGRAPHERS

Anderson, Larry 12, 13, 82, 96
Archbould, Cathie cover, 15, 16, 79, 108, 109, 111
Brend, Yvette 63, 116, 123
Cornelius, Don 1, 7, 45
Cornelius, Karen 22, 45, 120
Crandall, Alissa 12, 70, 105, 107, 112, 122
Daniels, Danny 69
Dick, Laurent 18, 19, 20, 28, 29, 37, 39, 42, 44, 112, 116, 117, 119

Doogan, Mike 71, 75, 81, 85
Flatten, Craig 16, 26
Hahn, Robert 14, 20, 21, 29, 115
Kerr, Leslie 46
Lotscher, Chlaus 24, 26, 31, 33, 36, 38, 48
Majiski, Joyce 32, 36, 118
Matz, George 11, 106
McCutcheon, Steve 61, 64, 65, 73, 74, 76, 77, 78, 87
McGovern-Rowen, Matt 36, 110
Montagna, Richard 4, 14, 24, 34
Nickles, Jon R. 3, 20
Rennick, Penny 115
Rhode, David 72
Soucek, Tom 21
Steele, Edward 22, 27, 113, 123
Walker, Harry M. 8, 17, 23, 25, 54, 107
Wuerthner, George 10, 12, 28, 35, 86, 95, 114, 121 ●

ALASKA GEOGRAPHIC Back Issues

The North Slope, Vol. 1, No. 1. Out of print.
One Man's Wilderness, Vol. 1, No. 2. Out of print.
Admiralty...Island in Contention, Vol. 1, No. 3. $19.95.
Fisheries of the North Pacific, Vol. 1, No. 4. Out of print.
Alaska-Yukon Wild Flowers, Vol. 2, No. 1. Out of print.
Richard Harrington's Yukon, Vol. 2, No. 2. Out of print.
Prince William Sound, Vol. 2, No. 3. Out of print.
Yakutat: The Turbulent Crescent, Vol. 2, No. 4. Out of print.
Glacier Bay: Old Ice, New Land, Vol. 3, No. 1. Out of print.
The Land: Eye of the Storm, Vol. 3, No. 2. Out of print.
Richard Harrington's Antarctic, Vol. 3, No. 3. $19.95.
The Silver Years, Vol. 3, No. 4. $19.95.
Alaska's Volcanoes, Vol. 4, No. 1. Out of print.
The Brooks Range, Vol. 4, No. 2. Out of print.
Kodiak: Island of Change, Vol. 4, No. 3. Out of print.
Wilderness Proposals, Vol. 4, No. 4. Out of print.
Cook Inlet Country, Vol. 5, No. 1. Out of print.
Southeast: Alaska's Panhandle, Vol. 5, No. 2. Out of print.
Bristol Bay Basin, Vol. 5, No. 3. Out of print.
Alaska Whales and Whaling, Vol. 5, No. 4. $19.95.
Yukon-Kuskokwim Delta, Vol. 6, No. 1. Out of print.
Aurora Borealis, Vol. 6, No. 2. $19.95.
Alaska's Native People, Vol. 6, No. 3. Out of print.
The Stikine River, Vol. 6, No. 4. $19.95.
Alaska's Great Interior, Vol. 7, No. 1. $19.95.
Photographic Geography of Alaska, Vol. 7, No. 2. Out of print.
The Aleutians, Vol. 7, No. 3. Out of print.
Klondike Lost, Vol. 7, No. 4. Out of print.
Wrangell-Saint Elias, Vol. 8, No. 1. Out of print.
Alaska Mammals, Vol. 8, No. 2. Out of print.
The Kotzebue Basin, Vol. 8, No. 3. Out of print.
Alaska National Interest Lands, Vol. 8, No. 4. $19.95.
Alaska's Glaciers, Vol. 9, No. 1. Revised 1993. $19.95.
Sitka and Its Ocean/Island World, Vol. 9, No. 2. Out of print.
Islands of the Seals: The Pribilofs, Vol. 9, No. 3. $19.95.
Alaska's Oil/Gas & Minerals Industry, Vol. 9, No. 4. $19.95.
Adventure Roads North, Vol. 10, No. 1. $19.95.
Anchorage and the Cook Inlet Basin, Vol. 10, No. 2. $19.95.
Alaska's Salmon Fisheries, Vol. 10, No. 3. $19.95.
Up the Koyukuk, Vol. 10, No. 4. $19.95.
Nome: City of the Golden Beaches, Vol. 11, No. 1. $19.95.

Alaska's Farms and Gardens, Vol. 11, No. 2. $19.95.
Chilkat River Valley, Vol. 11, No. 3. $19.95.
Alaska Steam, Vol. 11, No. 4. $19.95.
Northwest Territories, Vol. 12, No. 1. $19.95.
Alaska's Forest Resources, Vol. 12, No. 2. $19.95.
Alaska Native Arts and Crafts, Vol. 12, No. 3. $24.95.
Our Arctic Year, Vol. 12, No. 4. $19.95.
Where Mountains Meet the Sea, Vol. 13, No. 1. $19.95.
Backcountry Alaska, Vol. 13, No. 2. $19.95.
British Columbia's Coast, Vol. 13, No. 3. $19.95.
Lake Clark/Lake Iliamna, Vol. 13, No. 4. Out of print.
Dogs of the North, Vol. 14, No. 1. $19.95.
South/Southeast Alaska, Vol. 14, No. 2. Out of print.
Alaska's Seward Peninsula, Vol. 14, No. 3. $19.95.
The Upper Yukon Basin, Vol. 14, No. 4. $19.95.
Glacier Bay: Icy Wilderness, Vol. 15, No. 1. Out of print.
Dawson City, Vol. 15, No. 2. $19.95.
Denali, Vol. 15, No. 3. $19.95.
The Kuskokwim River, Vol. 15, No. 4. $19.95.
Katmai Country, Vol. 16, No. 1. $19.95.
North Slope Now, Vol. 16, No. 2. $19.95.
The Tanana Basin, Vol. 16, No. 3. $19.95.
The Copper Trail, Vol. 16, No. 4. $19.95.
The Nushagak Basin, Vol. 17, No. 1. $19.95.
Juneau, Vol. 17, No. 2. Out of print.
The Middle Yukon River, Vol. 17, No. 3. $19.95.
The Lower Yukon River, Vol. 17, No. 4. $19.95.
Alaska's Weather, Vol. 18, No. 1. $19.95.
Alaska's Volcanoes, Vol. 18, No. 2. $19.95.
Admiralty Island: Fortress of Bears, Vol. 18, No. 3. $19.95.
Unalaska/Dutch Harbor, Vol. 18, No. 4. $19.95.
Skagway: A Legacy of Gold, Vol. 19, No. 1. $19.95.
Alaska: The Great Land, Vol. 19, No. 2. $19.95.
Kodiak, Vol. 19, No. 3. $19.95.
Alaska's Railroads, Vol. 19, No. 4. $19.95.
Prince William Sound, Vol. 20, No. 1. $19.95.
Southeast Alaska, Vol. 20, No. 2. $19.95.
Arctic National Wildlife Refuge, Vol. 20, No. 3. $19.95.
Alaska's Bears, Vol. 20, No. 4. $19.95.
The Alaska Peninsula, Vol. 21, No. 1. $19.95.
The Kenai Peninsula, Vol. 21, No. 2. $19.95.

People of Alaska, Vol. 21, No. 3. $19.95.
Prehistoric Alaska, Vol. 21, No. 4. $19.95.
Fairbanks, Vol. 22, No. 1. $19.95.
The Aleutian Islands, Vol. 22, No. 2. $19.95.
Rich Earth: Alaska's Mineral Industry, Vol. 22, No. 3. $19.95.
World War II in Alaska, Vol. 22, No. 4. $19.95.
Anchorage, Vol. 23, No. 1. $21.95.
Native Cultures in Alaska, Vol. 23, No. 2. $19.95.
The Brooks Range, Vol. 23, No. 3. $19.95.
Moose, Caribou and Muskox, Vol. 23, No. 4. $19.95.
Alaska's Southern Panhandle, Vol. 24, No. 1. $19.95.
The Golden Gamble, Vol. 24, No. 2. $19.95.
Commercial Fishing in Alaska, Vol. 24, No. 3. $19.95.
Alaska's Magnificent Eagles, Vol. 24, No. 4. $19.95.
Steve McCutcheon's Alaska, Vol. 25, No. 1. $21.95.

PRICES AND AVAILABILITY SUBJECT TO CHANGE

Membership in The Alaska Geographic Society includes a subscription to *ALASKA GEOGRAPHIC*, the Society's colorful, award-winning quarterly.

Call or write for current membership rates or to request a free catalog. *ALASKA GEOGRAPHIC* back issues are also available (see above list). NOTE: This list was current in mid-1998. If more than a year or two have elapsed since that time, <u>please contact us before ordering to check prices and availability of specific back issues</u>.

When ordering back issues please add $4 for the first book and $2 for each additional book ordered for Priority Mail. Inquire for non-U.S. postage rates. To order, send check or money order (U.S. funds) or VISA/MasterCard information (including expiration date and your phone number) with list of titles desired to:

ALASKA GEOGRAPHIC
P.O. Box 93370 • Anchorage, AK 99509-3370
Phone: (907) 562-0164 • Fax (907) 562-0479

NEXT ISSUE:

Climbing Alaska, Vol. 25, No. 3

Climbers, guides and mountaineering experts uncover the mystique that draws thousands of people to Alaska's mountain ranges each year. This issue combines historical accounts of first ascents with contemporary climbing issues to provide an informative look at some of the world's most perilous peaks and those who dare to scale them. To members fall 1998.

ALASKA GEOGRAPHIC GUIDES

An ideal pocket reference for residents, travelers or inquiring minds, each book in this popular series is packed with reliable information, detailed maps and full-color photographs.

To order, phone (907) 562-0164, fax (907) 562-0479, or write to us at P.O. Box 93370-GA, Anchorage AK 99509-3370.